PUNISHMENT AND DETERRENCE

PUNISHMENT
AND
DETERRENCE

Johannes Andenaes

With a Foreword by Norval Morris

ANN ARBOR
THE UNIVERSITY OF MICHIGAN PRESS

ACKNOWLEDGMENTS

These articles are reprinted in adapted form from the following journals:

"General Prevention—Illusion or Reality?" is reprinted by permission from the *Journal of Criminal Law, Criminology and Political Science,* vol. 43, no. 2. Copyright © 1952 by Northwestern University School of Law.

"The General-Preventive Effects of Punishment" is reprinted by permission from the *University of Pennsylvania Law Review,* vol. 114, no. 7. © Copyright 1966 by the University of Pennsylvania.

"Deterrence and Specific Offenses" is reprinted by permission from *The University of Chicago Law Review,* vol. 38, no. 3. © 1971 by The University of Chicago.

"The Moral or Educative Influence of Criminal Law" and Appendix 3 are reprinted from *The Journal of Social Issues,* vol. 27, no. 2, 1971, by permission of The Society for the Psychological Study of Social Issues.

"The Morality of Deterrence" is reprinted by permission from *The University of Chicago Law Review,* vol. 37, no. 4. © 1970 by The University of Chicago.

"Does Punishment Deter Crime?" is partly reprinted with the new title, "General and Specific Deterrence," by permission of Canada Law Book Ltd. from *The Criminal Law Quarterly.*

FOREWORD

Serious analysis of the operation and efficacy of deterrent sanctions is essential to shaping an efficient and humane system of criminal justice. Those who approach this topic find that the writings of Johannes Andenaes tower over the works of others. Andenaes stimulated and deeply influenced all recent studies of deterrence, and his own current scholarship remains on the leading edge of our acquisition of knowledge of the legal threat as an inhibitor of criminal behavior.

It may be unfashionable, in the heated disputes that characterize so much contemporary public and professional discussion of crime and its control, to allow much weight to careful analysis of the deterrent purposes of the criminal justice system; yet deterrence remains a central purpose of criminal sanctions. If the criminal law is not in part a mechanism of deterrence, aiming to inhibit criminal conduct by the threat and actuality of punishment, why do we keep it at all? Rehabilitation, though rhetorically fashionable, cannot be a sufficient purpose of criminal sanctions. Why should we confine its benefits to convicted criminals? Many of the unconvicted manifestly stand in urgent need of reform. Why not coercively rehabilitate them too? Vengeance seems an atavistic aim, though doubtless it has a role. And we don't follow through on the segregation of offenders as an end in itself. Quite clearly, criminal sanctions are imposed with diverse purposes, and deterrence, within appropriate ethical constraints, is a leading and entirely proper objective of the criminal justice system.

Andenaes forced analysis beyond the simplistic questions of whether criminal sanctions deter or not—they clearly do in some cases—to a more complex and elusive series of empirical and ethical problems of deterrence in diverse criminal law efforts at behavioral control. He laid the conceptual, ethical, and analytical foundations for the hard empirical work that now begins—the assessment of the variables of certainty of punishment, celerity of punishment, and severity of punishment as they influence different categories of crimes, different categories of criminals, and different categories of punishments. This is a complex web of knowledge. To be clearly seen, one is wise to approach it with Andenaes as a guide.

Two of the essays in this book are already much cited in the literature, but their impact is greatly increased by their inclusion here with Andenaes' other and more recent studies. The overarching structure of his developing analysis of deterrence emerges for the first time in this collection; it can be neglected by no serious legislator, administrator or policy maker in the criminal law, and certainly by no scholar with hope of understanding the prevention and control of crime and delinquency.

All this sounds forbidding and possibly esoteric, but, in fact, Andenaes writes with a light touch and addresses hard philosophic issues in a pragmatic, no-nonsense, down-to-earth Scandinavian style. He argues without frills, without affectation, but without sacrifice of depth.

NORVAL MORRIS
University of Chicago
Center for Studies in Criminal Justice

CONTENTS

INTRODUCTION

The subject of deterrence is a highly controversial one. An American author said some time ago, somewhat ironically, that one of the basic principles learned by every student of criminology is that "punishment does not deter" (Jeffery, *Criminal Behavior and Learning Theory,* 56 J. CRIM. L.C. & P.S. 294 [1965]). On the other hand, a large part of the general public, politicians, police authorities, and judges seem to think very highly of the deterrent potentialities of criminal law. When I first wrote about the deterrent effects of criminal law twenty years ago it was under the heading: "General Prevention—Illusion or Reality?" When I returned to the subject many years later, in a General Report to the International Congress of Criminology in Montreal in 1965, I had become somewhat bolder. I ventured to drop the question mark, and in the summary of my report I stated that "the problem is not one of determining whether such effects exist; it is one of determining the conditions under which they occur and the degree to which they occur." This has become a recurrent theme in my various contributions to the subject, together with another one: The working of the criminal law must always be seen in its full cultural context. There is always a complicated interplay between the law and the multitude of other factors which shape our attitudes and behavior.

The papers collected in this volume represent a span of twenty years. The first paper, originally delivered at a meeting of the Norwegian Association of Criminalists, was of an exploratory character, an attempt to analyze the problem and confront sweeping statements with available experience. The second is an attempt to develop further the main ideas of the first in a more systematic way. The next three papers deal more fully with limited aspects of the subject. The first draft of these papers was made in 1968 during a stay at the Center for Studies in Criminal Justice at the University of Chicago, where I had the benefit of discussions with Norval Morris, Frank Zimring, and Gordon Hawkins. The last paper ("The Future of Criminal Law") which was first read to an English audience, transcends the subject of deterrence, but I trust that the attentive reader will discover the connections.

Apart from a few minor corrections, abridgments, and cross references, the papers are presented in the form they were first printed. I hope the resulting unavoidable overlapping will be found bearable. There are two exceptions from the principle. The paper on "The Moral or Educative Influence of Criminal Law" has been partly rewritten and expanded, and the latter part of the original paper is presented as *Appendix 3*. A paper "Does Punishment Deter Crime?", first published in the *Canadian Criminal Law Quarterly,* has been omitted from the collection in order to avoid too much duplication, but part of its content is presented in *Appendix 2*.

A question of terminology should be mentioned at the outset. The title of the book, as well as the titles of several of the papers, employ the term *deterrence*. In other papers the expression (general and special) *prevention* is used. A key to this seeming inconsistency is given in *Appendix 1*.

I

GENERAL PREVENTION—
ILLUSION OR REALITY?

The trend in penal reform in the past two generations has pointed in the direction of wider scope for individual prevention (specific prevention). As a result, the prosecuting authorities and the courts have, through the years, had an ever wider choice of sanctions put at their disposal, adapted to the personality of the offender. We now have special methods of treatment for juvenile delinquents, abnormal offenders, habitual criminals, vagrants, and alcoholics. These methods have been developed partly within and partly outside the framework of the penal system; hence they are partly punitive and partly non-punitive in nature. The catchword for the whole development is the well-known saying of Frantz von Liszt: It is not the crime but the criminal that is to be punished.

It would be an exaggeration to say that this development has proceeded without opposition. But the opposition has been far weaker than might be expected, inasmuch as most of those who consider the general-preventive function of penal law to be the core of the punitive system have felt they could make these concessions without any great danger.

But now and then conflict becomes apparent. It is especially among doctors and prison administrators that we often note great skepticism toward the belief in general prevention. Sometimes we see general prevention characterized as little better than a figment of the imagination, a fiction used by jurists as a defense for their traditional rules and concepts. "I shudder," says the Danish physician, Tage Kemp, director of Copenhagen University's Institute for Hereditary Biology, "when I think what this essentially fictitious concept has cost us, in terms of thousands upon thousands of wasted, bitter man-years of imprisonment— and how many lives it has ruined which could just as well have been saved. We lose much of our belief in the need for general prevention if, instead of looking upon the criminal cursorily, thinking in terms of dry, unrealistic legal formalism, we think in more individualistic terms, as indicated by the latest research in criminology and social biology."

Most jurists take a more positive attitude toward general prevention. Some go so far as to regard the general-preventive function as the only possible argument to support both punishment and the awarding of damages. Lundstedt is a good representative of this view; he in turn attacks the idea of individual prevention. "The idea that punishment aims at adjusting the criminal to society is surely one of the most fantastic to be found even in scholastic jurisprudence," he once wrote with an outspokenness characteristic of his style. "Experience teaches us that punishment has exactly the opposite effect on the criminal. Punishment has a natural tendency to demoralize the convicted person, and it frequently shunts him over to a class of social outcasts."

Even if there are not many who would go so far as Lundstedt, we can see jurists motivating their decisions with considerations of general prevention practically every day. This applies especially to lawmaking. In the premises to the Norwegian Penal Code of 1842 it is clearly stated: "The Theory of Deterrence, which in fact forms the basis for our present legislation . . . [appears] to be the main factor to be borne in mind in determining the nature and magnitude of punishments"—but as a secondary purpose there should also be consideration for the effect of punishment on the individual criminal, "in so far as attainment of the primary object permits this." The Penal Code of 1902 and the special laws passed in connection with it represent in many respects a victory for individual prevention. The father of the new law, Bernhard Getz, said in a lecture on the reform before the Norwegian Association of Criminalists that its aim was to "set up a whole system of institutions by which the state can seek to combat crime at its source or upon its manifestation in a manner adapted to each age group and category of crime." Notwithstanding a broader range of vision today than a century ago, I do not think I go far afield in maintaining that it is a primarily general-preventive consideration— having an eye to what is necessary to keep the people reasonably law-abiding—which today's legislators have in mind, too, when they define crimes and stipulate punishments. They defer somewhat to individual prevention, to be sure, by permitting the courts to set an appropriate punishment in each individual case.

General prevention often appears in judgments as well—especially in situations new to the courts, when they feel a need to offer a deeper explanation than simple reference to precedent.[1]

The controversial question of the general-preventive effect of punishment, therefore, is not merely of theoretical interest: it has a very practical side. And it is especially at the present time extremely important to shed light on the problem. Economic and political developments are responsible for legislation's interfering in the individual's affairs in quite a different way than previously—especially in economic matters. And the cure-all for enforcing these rules is threat of punishment. Thus we find a new category of offenses, whose social consequences can be even more dangerous than the more traditional crimes, but which are not regarded so in the public's moral judgment. Wherever legislation breaks new ground in this way, it becomes vital to learn the answers to questions like these: To what extent are we able to direct people's conduct by threat of punishment? What are the prerequisites for an effective legal prohibition? Can we, for example, maintain a prohibition which is not sanctioned by the public's moral code? How important is magnitude of penalty as compared with the risk of disclosure? What is the effect upon general respect for law of the state's sustaining prohibitions that are openly being disregarded?

It would be interesting to try to explain the reasons for the various attitudes toward general prevention in the various professional groups having contact with crime problems. It would require a rather extensive investigation into the specific views and the grounds given for them. But certain points are already evident. Prison officials and doctors naturally regard it as their chief function to help the individual who has come into conflict with the law to make a new start. By the emotional factor alone, this means a tendency to put the main emphasis on individual prevention, at the expense of the less tangible general prevention. The personal tragedies produced by punishment that is unnecessary or undesirable in terms of individual prevention can readily be perceived, while the indirect effects of punishment escape observation. Another point worth noting is that prison officials and mental examiners are constantly coming across cases where threat of punishment has been ineffective. It is understandable that this constantly recurring observation can induce skepticism as to the efficacy of threat of punishment. Where the mental examiner is concerned, there is also the point that the picture of crime he gets is dominated by the more or less abnormal personalities which it is his lot to deal with. The lawyer, on the other hand, often has little psychological insight and little acquaintance with the sort of persons who most frequently come into conflict with the law. So he can easily lose sight of the irrational factors in human motivation and construct psychologically superficial explanations, based on a view that crime grows out of conscious, rational consideration as to what is most profitable. Such reasoning leads naturally to Feuerbach's formula of psychological coercion: The risk for the lawbreaker must be made so great, the punishment so severe, that he knows he has more to lose than he has to gain from his crime.

So it is easy to find explanations for our problem by referring to the jobs and areas of experience of the different occupational groups. But I believe the differences are a bit more apparent than real. Perhaps they arise because the disputants attach different meanings to the terms "general prevention" and "individual prevention." Or perhaps they think of different types of offenders. The purpose of this paper is to contribute to a tidying up of the discussion.

Before I start my exposition I should perhaps pause for a moment to offer a precise definition of the concepts in question and their interrelationship.

By general prevention we mean the ability of criminal law and its enforcement to make citizens law-abiding. If general prevention were 100 percent effective there would be no crime at all. General prevention may depend on the mere frightening or deterrent effect of punishment—the risk of discovery and punishment outweighing the temptation to commit crime. This was what Feuerbach had in mind when he designed his famous theory of punishment as psychological coercion directed against the citizen. Later theory puts much stress on the ability of penal law to arouse or strengthen inhibitions of another sort. In Swedish discussion the *moralizing*—in other words the *educational*—function has been greatly stressed.[2] The idea is

that punishment as a concrete expression of society's disapproval of an act helps to form and to strengthen the
public's moral code and thereby creates conscious and unconscious inhibitions against committing crime. Unconscious inhibitions against committing forbidden acts can
also be aroused without appealing to the individual's concepts of morality. Purely as a matter of habit, with fear,
respect for authority, or social imitation as connecting
links, it is possible to induce favorable attitudes toward
this or that action and unfavorable attitudes toward another action. We find the clearest example of this in the
military, where extended inculcation of discipline and
stern reaction against breach thereof can induce a purely
automatic, habitual response—not only where obeying specific orders is concerned, but also with regard to general
orders and regulations. We have another example in the
relationship between an occupying power and an occupied
population. The regulations set down by the occupier are
not regarded by the people as morally binding; but by a
combination of terror and habit formation a great measure
of obedience can be elicited—at any rate in response to
commands which do not conflict too greatly with national
feelings.

We can say that punishment has three sorts of general-
preventive effects: it may have a *deterrent* effect, it may
strengthen *moral inhibitions* (a *moralizing* effect), and it
may stimulate *habitual law-abiding conduct*. I have reason
to emphasize this, since many of those who are most skeptical of general prevention think only of the deterrent effect.
Even if it can be shown that conscious fear of punishment
is not present in certain cases, this is by no means the same
as showing that the secondary effects of punishment are
without importance. To the lawmaker, the achievement of
inhibition and habit is of greater value than mere deterrence. For these apply in cases where a person need not
fear detection and punishment, and they can apply with-

out the person even having knowledge of the legal prohibition.

By individual prevention we mean the effect of punishment on the punished. At best this results in genuine moral improvement or in the acquisition of pro-social habits. Here the contrast to general prevention is quite clear. The same holds where the punished is rendered harmless—for good, by means of capital punishment or banishment, or temporarily by means of determinate prison sentences. In other cases the effect on the convict is simple deterrence, without any change in character being induced. When a motorist is fined $5.00 for illegal parking he is neither improved nor rendered harmless, but he will presumably be more careful the next time he parks. Thenceforth the motorist's thinking in such situations will be influenced both general-preventively and individual-preventively. The deterrent effect which the law by itself has on every citizen will be strengthened in his case by the fact that he knows from personal experience that the law means what it says.

The disagreement over the importance of general prevention is of course largely due to the fact that its effectiveness cannot be measured. We do not know the true extent of crime. In certain areas of crime there is reason to believe that the figures available for offenses which are prosecuted and punished corresponds roughly to the true incidence of crime. In other areas recorded crimes represent only a small fraction of the true incidence. We know still less about how many people *would* have committed crimes if there had been no threat of punishment. There is a certain lesson to be drawn from the events following upon changes in the law or in other circumstances important to general prevention—such as police efficiency. We can also get somewhere by the use of common sense and psychology. But even so, it can hardly be denied that any conclusion as to the real nature of general prevention involves a great deal of guesswork. Claims based on the "demands of general prevention," therefore, can often be used to cloak strictly retributive demands for punishment or mere conservative resistance to change. On the other hand, it is just as possible that the importance of general prevention is seriously overlooked by those who are mainly interested in a more efficacious treatment of the individual offender.

In our attempt to get a better understanding of the problem, it is of primary importance that we should not take all crime together but take each important group of crimes separately. One reason why the discussion on general prevention is often so fruitless, and why there is such sharp disagreement is, in my experience, that the protagonists generalize too much. They talk about general prevention in the general case, yet tend to draw from experience they have gained in particular areas. This is, in fact, a common error in legal discussions: on the basis of a limited material a theory is built to cover a much wider area than is logically justified. Psychological attitudes vary markedly in the different categories of law-breaking, and they can also vary markedly in different groups and strata of the society. As obvious as it is that it is impossible to do a criminological study throwing together thieves and murderers, rapists and usurers, swindlers and thugs, it should be just as obvious that a study of the general-preventive effect of punishment must also be differentiated. In a short paper like this it is, of course, not possible to give any more than samples from selected areas.

　1. I shall begin with a group of crimes which play a modest role in the literature but which have a good deal of practical importance and are good for illustration, all these *police regulations* which are such commonplaces in modern times: traffic ordinances, building codes, laws governing the sale of alcoholic beverages, regulations governing

commerce, etc. Here there is no doubt that punishment for infraction has primarily a general-preventive function. Here nearly all of us are potential criminals. A public-spirited citizen has, of course, certain inhibitions against breaking laws and regulations. But experience shows that moral and social inhibitions against breaking the law are not enough in themselves to insure obedience, where there is conflict with one's private interests. Thus the extent to which there can be effective enforcement by means of punishment determines to what extent the rules are actually going to be observed. As an example of rules which are just about 100 percent effective, because one must count on detection and punishment of all infractions, we can take blackout regulations during war. Deterrence alone suffices here, even without support of the moral authority which the law usually has. Consider a blacked-out city in an occupied country. The occupier's order has no moral authority at all—on the contrary, he is the enemy and must be resisted. But even so, hundreds of thousands of families take great care each night to prevent the least crack of light from showing. As if guided by an unseen hand, these countless householders go into action as soon as darkness falls. No one defies the order, because everyone knows that there is not enough to be gained to make the risk worthwhile. And eventually it becomes a habit, which is followed automatically, practically without thought. It would be hard to find a more impressive example of the "terror effect" of the threat of punishment under favorable circumstances.

It is not hard to find examples of the opposite: regulations which are not observed because there is no punishment of offenders against them. The Danish state prosecutor, Jörgen Trolle, has described the problem presented by Danish tourists to Sweden in an article in *Ugeskrift for Retsvæsen,* 1947 (Weekly Law Review).[3] There were no restrictions on travel to Sweden, although one could only buy a one-way ticket, not round trip. It was forbidden to take Danish or Swedish money out of Denmark, and this was strictly enforced; travelers were even searched occasionally. It was forbidden to borrow money in Sweden, and any assets already there were to be called home. The logical conclusion, says Trolle, was that traffic would be minimal, comprising only those few who could persuade the National Bank to sell them some Swedish currency or who had close and prosperous relatives in Sweden. But on the contrary, we witnessed great hordes, some days up to several thousand, crossing over to Sweden and returning laden down with goods. The travelers were so numerous that the customs officials and police had to throw up their hands. They checked to see if the travelers had tobacco or other highly dutiable items, but they did not bother to ask how they had got the Swedish money.

Trolle observes that "although everyone knows that the great majority of the numerous travelers who cross the Sound with a passport issued by the Ministry of Justice and on a ship belonging to the Ministry of Transport are lawbreakers, infringing Ministry of Trade regulations, nevertheless the customs officials, who are subject to the Ministry of Finance, and the police, who are subject to the Ministry of Justice, do nothing."

His conclusion is as follows: "It is unjust that the less law-abiding portion of the population should have advantages which the more conscientious ones are deprived of. And it taxes respect for law that everyone and his brother can see and can draw the lesson that one can with impunity allow oneself a wide margin in observing the law."

This is a good example of how undesirable it is to pass laws which cannot be enforced. It is a common failing in legislation. It is so natural to resort to threat of punishment when the authorities decide they want to channel the citizen's actions in one direction or another. The legislators probably realize that many will break the rules but reason that many will observe them, so that something, at least, will be gained. Looked at from the point of view of the individual administrative branch, this can be valid enough, but if the reasoning is followed first in one area and then in another, it can hardly fail to demoralize respect both for the law and for public authority. It makes sense, therefore, that certain thinkers have warned against this "inflation in the administration of criminal law."

I have cited two examples above to show the two extremes. In most cases the efficiency of law enforcement lies between them. How strict the enforcement must be to effect a reasonable degree of general prevention, a reasonable degree of obedience in a given area of administration, depends on many factors—including, how much a person stands to gain by breaking the law and from which strata of the society the law-breakers are recruited. For example, it makes a difference that it is not the same sort of people who break parking regulations and who break the regulations against drunkenness in public places.

2. The example of Danish tourists to Sweden has taken us, strictly speaking, outside the area of true police regulations and into a new area, which we can call *economic crimes*. I do not mean primarily the traditional crimes against property like theft, embezzlement, fraud and receiving stolen goods—I shall come back to these later. I refer here to crimes against governmental regulation of the economy: price violations, rationing violations, unlawful foreign exchange transactions, offenses against workers protection, disregard of quality standards, and so on. Psychologically we can also put customs and tax evasion in this group, although logically these crimes belong in the fraud category.

In time of war and crisis, economic crime of this sort can have immense importance to the nation. Outside Scandinavia we have drastic examples of the entire distribution of foodstuffs being disrupted because the goods find their way onto the black market. From postwar Germany, for instance, we have heard how the starving urban population roamed the countryside carrying their family treasures, with the hope of bartering a little food for themselves—food which the farmers withheld from the controlled channels of distribution. Even under fairly normal conditions, however, the political trend in Western Europe seems to be in the direction of more public control of the economy. If the trend continues, the problem of making these controls effective will become a paramount question in penal law—indeed, a question of far greater dimensions than the sort usually discussed in criminological circles. For whatever our opinion may be on the question of free versus controlled economy, there is no denying that ineffective regulation is the worst arrangement of them all.

Psychologically, the economic crimes tend to be rather clear-cut. A large number of the people who are affected by economic regulations or by the levying of taxes and fees feel no strong moral inhibition against infraction. They often find excuses for their behavior in political theorizing: they oppose the current government's regulative policies; they find taxes unreasonably high; and they find support for such views in their newspapers, which daily represent the state as a great vampire and governmental agencies as business enemy number one. Yet the matter of obedience or disobedience can often have important economic consequences. It is to be expected that many will calculate in cold blood the risk of being caught, and act accordingly. It is rather significant that a Norwegian religious newspaper of January 1949 carried an article with roughly the following headline: "Time for Taxpayers to Prepare their Annual Evasion." In this area, at any rate, Feuerbach's law of general prevention has a certain validity: it is necessary that consideration as to the risk involved in breaking the law should outweigh consideration of the advantages to breaking the law. The amount of threat needed varies greatly, of course, from person to person. One is a timid, cautious type; another likes to take chances. One has a social position he is afraid to lose; another has no such fear. Generally speaking, the biggest crimes in this area are committed by people with a certain economic and social position, people who can be deterred by even a rather modest risk of detection and punishment. When they break the law nevertheless, it is because they reckon it as overwhelmingly probable that all will go well.

In this connection we might consider what happened upon the calling in of paper money and the forced registration of bank accounts and securities in Norway in 1945.[4] Enormous values came to light which had previously escaped assessment. In some districts only a small percent of the actual bank holdings had previously been declared. On the basis of the registration we can almost lay down the rule that everyone was a tax evader who could be so without risk. The result is striking confirmation of what we could have inferred by ordinary psychological reasoning: the importance of policing to the enforcement of penal provisions. If there were such policing as to produce a risk of 25 percent in making false tax declarations, tax evasion on a grand scale would be practically eliminated.

From this reasoning I draw the following significant conclusion: in discussions on the introduction of new economic regulations, the question of the feasibility of effective enforcement should occupy a central place. And if it is found that such policing is not feasible, that the law will in effect reward dishonesty, the lawmakers should think twice and three times before legislating it—no matter how fine it looks on paper.

3. When we come to the traditional crimes against property, the picture is a bit more complicated. Strong

moral and social inhibitions against the criminal act appear alongside regard for the penal code. Now the question is: Are not these moral and social inhibitions enough in themselves to keep most people from committing thefts, frauds, and so on? And then: Will these moral and social inhibitions retain their strength if the risk of punishment is removed? Is not the methodical use of punishment or other forms of reaction as an answer to such infractions of the law one of the most important factors in arousing the public's taboo attitude toward them?

The question here is not whether you or I would remain law-abiding even if there were no "switch behind the back." The question is whether there is not a fairly large group on the moral borderline who might go wrong, and whether they might not in turn draw others with them. What we are concerned with is, of course, a long-term process, where the full effect of a weakening in the judicial reaction to crime will not be felt before the passage of a generation or more.

In discussing these questions we must not overlook the fact that for numerically important groups, especially in the cities, the social reaction against crime means little, because the moral standard in these groups is too low to be of account. Likewise we must not overlook the fact that the social reaction is connected in many ways to the judicial. This means not simply that general behavior with regard to a category of acts is affected by the law's attitude toward them: but also that *it would be much easier to keep one's acts secret and thus avoid all social reprobation, if one did not have to consider the risk of their being brought to public notice through criminal prosecution.*

The exceptional conditions that prevailed during the German occupation have given us new and valuable experience, even if it must be evaluated cautiously.

In Denmark the Germans arrested the entire Danish police force in September 1944. During the rest of the occupation the policing was done by an improvised and unarmed watch corps, which was all but ineffectual except when the criminal was caught red-handed. Jörgen Trolle headed the Copenhagen state prosecutor's office at the time, and in an extremely interesting book, *Syv Maaneder uden Politi* (Seven Months without Police), he has described what happened. The crime rate rose immediately, but there was wide discrepancy here between the various types of crime. While in the whole of 1939 only ten cases of robbery were reported in Copenhagen, the figure by 1943 had risen to ten a month, as a result of wartime conditions. After the action against the police the figure quickly rose to over 100 a month and continued to rise. Theft insurance payments quickly rose ten-fold and more. The fact that punishment was greatly increased for criminals who were caught and brought before the court could not prevent this. Crimes like embezzlement and fraud, where the perpetrator is generally known, do not seem to have increased notably.

As Trolle points out, every big city has its quota of underworld types who will exploit the opportunity given them by a crippling of the law enforcement system. In the next round, new circles will be drawn into crime, weak persons who are tempted when they see crimes go unpunished. The experiment in Denmark was imperfect and of short duration. What would happen if the state's punishing function were discontinued completely and for a rather long period can only be guessed. My own opinion is that such a complicated mechanism as a modern industrial society can hardly be kept going without police and penal courts. The gangster syndicates in America between the first and second World Wars show how powerful organized crime can become, when conditions are right for it. Just imagine what would have happened if the state had not stepped in resolutely with police, penal courts, and other measures, so that the gangs would have had free play: The individual law-abiding citizen would have been helpless, not only against the existing gangs, but against any new-comer who wanted to equip himself with a revolver and try his luck. If we carry the reasoning further, we can imagine how the big gangs would have found it profitable to divide the country among themselves, hauling in money by assessing the population and in return providing it with a certain security by cracking down on upstart competitors. There were actually strong tendencies in this direction. The existing society would have succumbed, and a new one would have risen to take its place—this would have corresponded remarkably to the Marxist definition of the state as a power combination whose purpose is to safeguard the ruling class' exploitation of the oppressed!

The Danish experiment is instructive, but such a radi-cal crippling of law enforcement will hardly be experienced under normal conditions. To illustrate the way demorali-zation spreads as a result of slack law enforcement under more normal conditions, I can refer to something that happened here in Norway a number of years ago and caused a small sensation. There had been thieving from a military arsenal over a fairly long period of time. It ended finally in violence, as a watchman was shot and killed by two boys caught in the act of breaking in. Now the police got busy; there were house searches and many arrests. Great quantities of stolen goods were recovered. Accord-ing to newspaper accounts, whole truckloads of stolen mili-tary goods were rounded up—weapons, ammunition, radio sets, telephone equipment, fur coats, tarpaulins, search-lights, saddles, uniforms and helmets. And here I quote a newspaper report based on information given by the police and concluding with an analysis into the cause of the thefts:

> There is no escaping the fact that the thefts were entirely due to poor guarding. The boys all say they heard from comrades how easy it was to steal from the arsenal, and so

they went out and tried it. It is characteristic that most of the boys know the names of the two 'watchdogs,' and that none were afraid of them. The lax guarding at the main arsenal became known to all the boys; when some tried to break in, and it went well every time, the thieving gained momentum.

Such a development is no rarity. The process is as follows: Some begin to steal because it is easy and safe. Others hear about it and try their luck, too. The bigger the group implicated, the less each individual in it is able to feel he is doing anything wrong. In the above case it was a question of state property, to boot, which people seem to have comparatively little respect for. But it would hardly have made any great difference if the stores had belonged to a private firm instead.

4. When we look at *moral offenses,* we find there are entirely different factors to be dealt with. The urge for economic gain is a universal motive for crime, even if its intensity varies from case to case. Practically no one can claim to be entirely immune to the temptations of Mammon. Many sex offenses, on the other hand, grow out of abnormal or unharmonious sexual adjustments. Homosexuality, exhibitionism, sexual assaults on children, incest, and the like, have no appeal for the normal personality. The scope of general prevention is thus here limited to those few people who because of their sex impulses are especially vulnerable. At the same time, these acts are strongly disapproved socially, so that mere anticipation of discovery affords a powerful deterrent. And because the acts are determined by sex impulses, often being performed as outlets for strong mental tensions, the psychological mechanism is quite different from that at work, for instance, in the economic crimes which I have discussed above.

For this and for other reasons, sex offenses belong in the area of crime where there is reason to be somewhat skeptical about the general-preventive validity of threat of punishment. It might be noted, incidentally, that the amount of rape and other sex offenses did not appear to increase particularly during the policeless period in Copenhagen. It is hard to calculate, however, what the effect of slackness in enforcement would be in the long run. In all probability the effect would be quite different for the different offenses. In some countries, such as France, incest is usually unpunishable. Whether this has had any influence on the prevalence of incest cannot, of course, be determined with any exactness. But there is at least nothing to indicate that such intercourse has become commonplace. That rape, on the other hand, is a crime not alien to the normal human personality, can be verified in times of war and occupation. In an occupation army where discipline in this matter is lax, the incidence of rape is commonly high. If discipline is strict, on the other hand, as with the German army of occupation in Norway during the war, the crime hardly ever occurs.

5. The reader probably expects me to take up *murder* next. To mystery story writers—and often to criminologists as well—murder is the crime par excellence. Criminology is mainly the study of murder. But in the every-day administration of justice in Scandinavia murder plays an extremely modest role. In the decade 1931–1940, forty-three persons were convicted of first degree murder in Norway, or four to five per year, about one-tenth of a percent of all criminal convictions. And motivation varies so markedly that it is impossible to evaluate the effect of criminal law in this area without further differentiation than there is space for here. The holdup man who kills simply for gain, the sex murderer whose crime assuages the darkest drives of his sick mind, the uxoricide who seeks desperate relief for a mental torment that is more than he can bear—there is a world of difference between these types; all they have in common is the judicial name for the

act. I could hardly do better here than quote Stephens'
famous words of 1863:

> Some men, probably, abstain from murder because they
> fear that if they committed murder they would be
> hanged. Hundreds of thousands abstain from it because
> they regard it with horror. One great reason why they re-
> gard it with horror is that murderers are hanged with the
> hearty approbation of all reasonable men.

6. A similar difficulty greets us as we attempt to
evaluate the general-preventive usefulness of threatening
punishment for rebellion, treason, and other political
crimes. There can be little doubt that the provisions
against treason, for example, have a certain moral weight
in emphasizing the extremely reprehensible nature of
treason and thereby inducing an attitude of repugnance
toward oneself committing the crime; but here as else-
where the effect is not really ascertainable. It is also evident that the risk element may affect the opportunist who
coldbloodedly calculates which course of action will be
most profitable. On the other hand, it is often said that
threat of punishment has no effect on the "genuine" political criminal, who is impelled by belief in the justice
of his cause. That can be true enough for some, but hardly
for the great mass of people to whom such political movements direct their appeal. To take an example from
nineteenth-century Norwegian history: the prosecution
of Marcus Thrane—the socialist agitator whose remains
have only recently been returned to Norway from America
to be interred with full official honors—completely crip-
pled the movement he had founded. The labor movement's later progress had nothing to do with this pioneer
movement. From the dictatorships of our own times we
know that it is possible for a brutal, relentless police system to eliminate all organized resistance to the regime. By
accompanying the political trials with a vigorous propa-

ganda, it may also be possible to induce a conviction in the people that such resistance is morally wrong. I am of course not proposing that these examples be followed: I mention them simply to show that punishment can be a deterrent and a moral force in this area as well.

It must be admitted, of course, that these uses of penal provisions are highly dependent upon the political balance of power, and on many other circumstances. During an enemy occupation threat of punishment against traitors will have little weight for those who feel certain that the occupier will win the war. And in certain cases—e.g. after a civil war—it can happen that prosecution of the rebels will not increase respect for the state's authority, but indeed perpetuate a split, in a way that can have serious repercussions. In such cases it can become difficult for the lawmakers to decide which is wiser: to overlook the crime by resorting to a partial or general amnesty, or to hold the guilty ones responsible to the fullest extent of the law.

Up to now I have intentionally avoided the question, in what way the general-preventive effect depends on the *nature and magnitude* of the reaction. In some respects this is the most immediate side of the problem. The magnitude of punishment is a factor which the lawmakers and the courts can regulate as they see fit, while it is harder for them to vary the other factors that are important— notably the intensity of policing and the set of mind of the public. The simplest way to make people more law-abiding, therefore, is to increase the punishment. When a certain type of crime threatens to get out of hand— blackout infringements or black market trading in war-time, for instance—the authorities often resort to stiffening the penal provisions. And when the courts are faced with the question of general prevention, they usually regard the choice as one between severe and light sentences in the individual case.

The best known example in modern Norwegian experience of such reasoning is the increased punishment for sex offenses called for in the penal code revision of 1927. The motive for the change was primarily general-preventive. The reasoning was that the sex offenses were becoming more numerous, and this was thought to be due to laxness on the part of the courts. But the effect of the change as reflected in crime statistics was astonishing. Instead of the decline in sex offenses that was expected, there was a notable rise. Comparing the five-year period before the change with the five-year period after the change, the average rose from 136 sex crimes per year to 229, or a rise of 68 percent. In the following years the figure has remained at about this level.

The example hardly tells us much about the general-preventive effect of threat of punishment, but it does show how careful we must be in drawing conclusions from the ordinary crime statistics. The figures for other crimes remained fairly constant in these years, and regardless of what we may think of the efficacy of harsh sentences in preventing crime, we certainly cannot conclude that they increase it. The explanation for the rise in incidence must be that this group of crimes now received more attention than before. The discussion and agitation that went with the revision and the stricter view that the new provisions gave expression to, doubtless caused many sex offenses that would not have been reported before to be reported now—and perhaps the police now investigated such cases more energetically as well. That this must be the explanation is supported by a glance at a breakdown of the statistics on sex offenses: the rise is found overwhelmingly in the types of cases that one would assume would often go unreported or unsolved—e.g. illicit relations with girls fourteen to sixteen years old.

If we think first of the purely deterrent value of threat of punishment—and with certain penal provisions this is the main point, as we have seen—it is clear that deterrence depends not simply on the risk of being punished, but also on the nature and magnitude of punishment. How important this factor is depends on the characteristic motivation for the crime, and on many other circumstances. Magnitude of punishment should mean more for crimes usually committed after careful consideration pro and con (e.g. tax evasion or smuggling of foreign currencies) than for crimes which grow out of emotions or drives which overpower the individual (e.g. the so-called crimes of passion). Another point is the moral condemnation attached to the deed. If this is strong, the magnitude of punishment is of minor importance. The social position of the potential criminal, incidentally, is also a factor. Embezzlement, for instance, is a crime which is often committed by persons in responsible positions and having some social prestige. To the respectable cashier, fear of detection is more fear of shame and scandal, and economic and social ruin, than it is fear of the punishment itself. Such a view is certainly alien to the bootlegger, however, for whom threat of punishment is just one of the risks of the trade.

That maximum deterrence does not follow from the severest punishment even Örsted, the great Danish legal thinker of a century ago, was able to point out, in his treatise "On the First Rules of Criminal Law." He shows how a penal system which the citizens and the administrators themselves regard as cruel will lead them to hold a protecting hand over the criminal rather than to cooperate in bringing him to justice. "With general enmity toward the penal code, it will lose its force, and impunity will be the real consequence of the law's always threatening the most severe punishment." Modern experience—e.g. the tendency of the jury to acquit when it fears that a verdict of guilty will mean too severe punishment for the defendant —confirm the correctness of Örsted's reasoning.

Turning next to the moral, the educative value of punishment, we find that magnitude of punishment is of importance here too. Punishment is an expression of society's disapproval of the act, and the degree of disapproval is expressed by the magnitude of punishment. A serious crime must be answered with a severe punishment, a minor misdemeanor with a lenient reaction. But here it is rather a question of the *relative* severity of the punishment than of its absolute magnitude. The humanizing of penal law in the past generations has led to a marked lowering of the general level of punishment. What was punishment for a minor crime a century ago is today punishment for a major crime. So long as this development does not take place faster than the public has a chance to adjust its ideas on appropriate punishment, it need have little effect on the ability of punishment to express society's disapproval. It is the same as with marks in school: the same mark can be expressed on a scale from 1 to 2 as on a scale from 1 to 6 or on one from 1 to 100. But a transition from one scale to another can cause some confusion.

A question of practical importance in this connection is: Can the law influence the public's attitude toward a group of punishable acts by changing their position on the marking scale? In other words, by increasing the punishment for a group of crimes can we not only increase its deterrent effect but also increase the moral inhibitions against them? It is impossible to say for sure. Personally, I think it probable that such an influence can occur in certain areas and to a limited degree, but that it is at best a long-term proposition. A deterrent effect can be achieved quickly; a moral effect takes longer.

These views on the relationship between general prevention and the magnitude of punishment are built upon abstract reasoning. No doubt there are some skeptical readers who are impatient to ask: Can you give any practical examples in which the magnitude of punishment has had influence on its general-preventive effect?

It must be admitted at once that only very little support for the proposition is to be educed from experience—in the first place because the general-preventive effect is always hard to ascertain, and second because there has never been a systematic gathering of material which could illuminate the question. I believe I can, however, give a few examples by way of illustration.

Normally it cannot be shown that it makes any difference to crime whether death or life imprisonment is the maximum penalty which can be imposed.[5] But that there are situations in which the death sentence can have a distinctly different effect than other punishments became apparent during the occupation. The great majority of the people came to feel that it was nationally and morally right to sabotage the occupation authorities. Thus no social opprobrium went with being arrested for illegal activity—quite the contrary. And toward the end of the occupation, when the duration was being reckoned in weeks and months, even the threat of life imprisonment became just a question of short internment. The only thing that could really worry a member of the underground was the thought of torture or death. I remember so well the day in October, 1942, when the *Reichskommissar* issued his ordinance promising death for having any traffic at all with illegal newspapers. There were many that day who got to work tidying up their effects, and the production and distribution of illegal newspapers suffered a serious setback. It was not long, however, before people realized that the ordinance was not to be taken seriously, and activity was resumed. Experience during the war also showed how the risk affects people differently according to their individual attitudes and sensitivity to danger. A large share of the population was unwilling to take any risk—they were against the Germans, to be sure, but their main consideration was their own pockets. Another large share was willing to take part in illegal work where the risk was small, and especially where they would not be risking their lives. A third group, numerically smaller and the heart of the resistance movement, was not to be deterred at all by risk.

All this is of a certain practical value in planning the treatment to be accorded revolutionary movements whose members can be assumed to have about the same attitude toward the lawful authorities as the majority of the Norwegian people had toward the Germans during the occupation. In their recent proposal for a revision of the treason and rebellion paragraphs of the Penal Code, the Norwegian Penal Code Commission has described what might happen if an armed rebellion should be started while the international situation is tense: "If the rebellion is not at once suppressed, it can easily lead to intervention by a foreign power. Then the situation might arise where there is reason to think that a death sentence against a leader of the rebellion is the only way to bring others to their senses and thereby win mastery of the situation for the lawful authorities."

Another practical example of the preventive value of heavy punishment is enactment of a rule in Norway calling for prison sentences without access to probation in cases of drunken driving. The subject is so familiar that it hardly requires elaboration. Most Norwegians are able to see on looking about their own circle of friends that it is becoming more common to leave the car at home when going to a party at which alcohol is likely to be consumed. There is unquestionably a certain preventive effect at work here. How great it is, and how it is distributed over the different social groups among motorists, and whether it is due simply to the deterrent effect or whether the law has succeeded in bringing about a change in attitude toward driving while intoxicated: All this is something we have no exact knowledge of; it could well be made the subject of a sociological study.

I have given a couple of examples of the effect of especially heavy sentences.[6] The other side of the question is whether special leniency to certain groups of offenders might not undermine respect for the law.

Attorney General Aulie, in his lecture on youthful offenders before the Association of Norwegian Criminalists in 1947, touched upon gangsterism, which is so typical in juvenile delinquency. He said:

> We know from experience that when members of the gang are released after questioning pending the winding up of investigation, the young people almost invariably flock back together, usually with the idea of planning new escapades. They regard the intervention of the police as a temporary inconvenience of negligible importance. They count on prosecution being waived for those with clean records, or at worst their being given suspended sentences. And they have reason to believe that a dozen or so new thefts on top of those already counted against them will not make much difference if they are discovered.

If this observation is correct, it shows with all desirable clarity that the humanizing of penal practice must be kept within certain limits if it is not to lead to an undermining of respect for law and authority. But it would take us far afield to go into this problem here.

With the last example I come to the relation between general and individual prevention. Usually there is no great conflict between the two. This is clearly the case when measures designed for individual prevention go farther than punishment designed along general-preventive lines—such as in the case of forced labor for vagrants and alcoholics or indeterminate sentences for recidivists. Such long sentences are, of course, sufficient for deterrence. Neither are they objectionable from the point of view of the moralizing function of punishment—at any rate, when it is clear to citizens that there is no question here of retribution for the crime but rather of a measure which aims to educate the prisoner or render him harmless. There is greater objection from a general-preventive point of view when individual considerations motivate an especially lenient treatment. But neither here should there be any real danger, so long as the milder special treatment does not become such a commonplace that the potential criminal can count on it and behave accordingly. Both the deterrent and the moralizing sides of general prevention are based primarily on the *average* reaction to certain offenses. Waiving of prosecution and the use of suspended sentence are so widely practiced that the conflict here has become acute.

More common than an out-and-out conflict between individual and general prevention is the circumstance that a punishment that is necessary for general prevention is often superfluous for individual prevention. In certain crimes there will practically never be an individual-preventive need for punishment—or at any rate, not a severe punishment: such things as perjury (so few persons are called in as witnesses more than once in a lifetime), or bigamy. In other cases the circumstances governing the behavior of the individual offender may lead to the conclusion that punishment is not needed for his benefit—"that execution of the sentence is not necessary to prevent the offender from committing new crimes," to quote the Penal Code's §52 on conditions for probation.

Thus the judge is often put in a difficult position. A single judgment has, to be sure, seldom any concrete effect on general prevention. The question is: Would general prevention be significantly impaired if it became the practice to apply probation or minimum sentence in similar cases? Something else to think about is whether people are likely to learn of the decisions and let their conduct be guided by them.

This problem came up in a treason case after the war.[7]

A young man was charged with having served in the German army—in itself a serious crime, meriting several years at hard labor. In this case, however, the circumstances were unusual. The defendant, who was still under twenty, was arrested by the Germans during the war and put into a concentration camp as a hostage for his mother, who had fled to Sweden. He felt depressed while in the camp and hit on the idea of getting out by volunteering for German war service and then escaping. He had, in fact, heard of people getting out in this way. He volunteered and was accepted, but for a while he was unable to escape. He was sent to Germany and then to serve six months at the front. But when he came home on leave at the end of 1944 he seized the opportunity to flee to Sweden.

In the lower court the defendant got a suspended sentence of one year's imprisonment. The majority in the Supreme Court, however, reversed the sentence. The writer of the majority opinion held that for the sake of precedent it was indefensible to let a person who had been guilty of such a desperate act as to join the enemy's army get by with a suspended sentence. The reasoning is psychologically a bit unrealistic. One justice dissented, holding that the use of probation in a single case which is clearly different from the majority of cases cannot be said to weaken the future preventive value of the reckoning with Norway's traitors. "This would presuppose knowledge in the future not only of the general lines of the present reckoning, but of its details—a knowledge which is theoretically possible in isolated cases, but which in my opinion can be disregarded in practice."

More than 70 years ago Lombroso wrote his famous book, *L'Uomo delinquente*, based on a study of prisoners in Italian penal institutions. Not many of his conclusions have stood the test of time. Most have been rejected as fanciful hypotheses and untenable generalizations. But he was a pioneer in his use of the empirical method in investigating the causes of crime. Psychiatrists, anthropologists, sociologists, and others have continued his work. An enormous body of empirical data has been amassed to aid in appraising lawbreakers' physical and mental traits, family conditions, economic position, and so on. As a result every generalizing theory has had to be abandoned. The time for broad slogans in criminology has passed.

No comparable empirical study of the psychology of *obedience to law* has been undertaken. In a word, we are still in the pre-Lombrosian era in this field. And the discussion often gives way to cock-sure general statements like "I believe (or I do not believe) in general prevention." Much has been written about general prevention; much talented effort has been spent in exploring its operation and importance. But the empirical data are still lacking. If any attempt has been made to include it at all, it has usually—as in this paper—occurred by the use of chance observations, plus ordinary psychological theories. I believe we can make some progress in this way. But we shall not have firm ground to stand on before a systematic investigation is made into the effect of penal law and its enforcement on the citizen's behavior, and into the interrelation between the legal system and the other factors which govern behavior. This task is in a sense much more difficult than the one Lombroso undertook. He had his material nicely collected and concentrated for him in the state prisons. One who wishes to study general prevention, on the other hand, must examine the whole population. Therefore it is a field for sociologists and psychologists. And it is difficult for one uninitiated into sociological methods of research to judge how the work should be tackled, or how far it is at all possible to go. I, at any rate, do not feel qualified to enlarge on the matter for the time being. But in this paper I have tried to point out how important these problems are.

Notes

1. On general-preventive considerations in sentencing, see chapter 5, "The Morality of Deterrence."

2. For a fuller discussion see chapter 4, "The Moral or Educative Influence of Criminal Law."

3. Just after the war Sweden was a land of plenty compared to Denmark, and some Danes used to take the two-hour boat trip across the Sound to buy scarce commodities. In the Swedish vernacular they became known as "locusts."—TRANS.

4. This was a measure, also resorted to in other European countries, to flush out ill-gotten gain from the war. The idea was that all liquid assets would have to be declared, and the tax authorities and investigators of economic treason would be able to trap profiteers—since the alternative to declaring the assets was to let them become worthless.—TRANS.

5. In Dano-Norwegian legal history there is one remarkable example of the death penalty being abandoned because it defeated its purpose in a certain type of crime. The Ordinance of December 18, 1767, replaced the death penalty with penal servitude for life in cases where "melancholy and other dismal persons [committed murder] for the exclusive purpose of losing their lives." The background for the provision was, in the words of Örsted, "the thinking that was then current among the unenlightened that by murdering another person and thereby being sentenced to death, one might still attain salvation, whereas if one were to take one's own life, one would be plunged into eternal damnation." (EUNOMIA, Part III, p. 147).

6. In discussion of this paper a participant (Police Chief Rode) cited as another example of the significance of magnitude of punishment for prevention his experience with smuggling during prohibition. In his district at least, rum running was dealt a severe blow after the courts began to adjudge prison sentences instead of fines.

The effect was not alone deterrent: the change was important also to the public's attitude toward crime. Prison, as opposed to fines, was regarded as shameful, and while smuggling had previously been looked upon as a thrilling sport, which even "decent citizens" could engage in, it now became something to stay away from.

7. The NORWEGIAN CASE REVIEW (*Norsk Retstidende*) 854 (1946).

II

THE GENERAL-PREVENTIVE EFFECTS
OF PUNISHMENT

"For what mortal is righteous if he nothing fear?"
(Aeschylus in the Eumenides)

THE CONCEPT OF GENERAL PREVENTION

In continental theories of criminal law, a basic distinction is
made between the effects of punishment on the man being
punished—individual prevention or special prevention—
and the effects of punishment upon the members of society
in general—general prevention. The characteristics of
special prevention are termed "deterrence," "reformation"
and "incapacitation," and these terms have meanings similar to their meanings in the English-speaking world. General prevention, on the other hand, may be described as the
*restraining influences emanating from the criminal law
and the legal machinery.*

By means of the criminal law, and by means of specific
applications of this law, "messages" are sent to members of
a society. The criminal law lists those actions which are
liable to prosecution, and it specifies the penalties involved. The decisions of the courts and actions by the police and prison officials transmit knowledge about the law,
underlining the fact that criminal laws are not mere empty

threats, and providing detailed information as to what kind of penalty might be expected for violations of specific laws. To the extent that these stimuli restrain citizens from socially undesired actions which they might otherwise have committed, a general preventive effect is secured. While the effects of special prevention depend upon how the law is implemented in each individual case, general prevention occurs as a result of an interplay between the provisions of the law and its enforcement in specific cases. In former times, emphasis was often placed on the physical exhibition of punishment as a deterrent influence, for example, by performing executions in public. Today it is customary to emphasize the *threat* of punishment as such. From this point of view the significance of the individual sentence and the execution of it lies in the support that these actions give to the law. It may be that some people are not particularly sensitive to an abstract threat of penalty, and that these persons can be motivated toward conformity only if the penalties can be demonstrated in concrete sentences which they feel relevant to their own life situations.

The effect of the criminal law and its enforcement may be *mere deterrence*. Because of the hazards involved, a person who contemplates a punishable offense might not act. But it is not correct to regard general prevention and deterrence as one and the same thing. The concept of general prevention also includes the *moral* or *socio-pedagogical* influence of punishment. The "messages" sent by law and the legal processes contain factual information about what would be risked by disobedience, but they also contain proclamations specifying that it is *wrong* to disobey. Some authors extend the concept of deterrence so that it includes the moral influences of the law and is, thus, synonymous with general prevention.[1] In this article, however, the term deterrence is used in the more restrictive sense.

The moral influence of the criminal law may take various forms. It seems to be quite generally accepted among the members of society that the law should be obeyed even though one is dissatisfied with it and wants it changed. If this is true, we may conclude that the law as an institution itself to some extent creates conformity. But more important than this formal respect for the law is respect for the values which the law seeks to protect. It may be said that from law and the legal machinery there emanates a flow of propaganda which favors such respect. Punishment is a means of expressing social disapproval. In this way the criminal law and its enforcement supplement and enhance the moral influence acquired through education and other nonlegal processes. Stated negatively, the penalty neutralizes the demoralizing consequences that arise when people witness crimes being perpetrated.

Deterrence and moral influence may both operate on the conscious level. The potential criminal may deliberate about the hazards involved, or he may be influenced by a conscious desire to behave lawfully. However, with fear or moral influence as an intermediate link, it is possible to create unconscious inhibitions against crime, and perhaps to establish a condition of habitual lawfulness. In this case, illegal actions will not present themselves consciously as real alternatives to conformity, even in situations where the potential criminal would run no risk whatsoever of being caught.

General-preventive effects do not occur only among those who have been informed about penal provisions and their applications. Through a process of learning and social imitation, norms and taboos may be transmitted to persons who have no idea about their origins—in much the way that innovations in Parisian fashions appear in the clothing of country girls who have never heard of Dior or Lanvin.

Making a distinction between special prevention and

general prevention is a useful way of calling attention to the importance of legal punishment in the lives of members of the general public, but the distinction is also to some extent an artificial one. The distinction is simple when one discusses the reformative and incapacitative effects of punishment on the individual criminal. But when one discusses the deterrent effects of punishment the distinction becomes less clear. Suppose a driver is fined ten dollars for disregarding the speed limit. He may be neither reformed nor incapacitated but he might, perhaps, drive more slowly in the future. His motivation in subsequent situations in which he is tempted to drive too rapidly will not differ fundamentally from that of a driver who has not been fined; in other words a general-preventive effect will operate. But for the driver who has been fined, this motive has, perhaps, been strengthened by the recollection of his former unpleasant experience. We may say that a general-preventive feature and special-preventive feature here act together.

Let me hasten to point out here that so far I have only presented a kind of conceptual framework. Determination of the extent to which such general-preventive effects exist, and location of the social conditions that are instrumental in creating them, are empirical problems which will be discussed in this paper.

A NEGLECTED FIELD OF RESEARCH

General prevention has played a substantial part in the *philosophy of the criminal law*. It is mentioned in Greek philosophy, and it is basic in the writings of Beccaria, Bentham, and Feuerbach. According to Feuerbach, for example, the function of punishment is to create a "psychological coercion" among the citizens.[2] The threat of penalty, consequently, had to be specified so that, in the mind of the potential malefactor, the fear of punishment carried more weight than did the sacrifice involved in refraining from the offense. The use of punishment in individual cases could be justified only because punishment was necessary to render the threat effective. The earlier writers were concerned mainly with the purely deterrent effects of punishment, while the moral effect of punishment has been subjected to detailed analysis in more recent theories, especially in Germany and in the Scandinavian countries.[3]

Notions of general prevention also have played a major part in *legislative actions*. This was especially apparent a hundred or a hundred and fifty years ago when the classical school was dominant. The Bavarian Penal Code of 1813, copied by many countries, was authored by Feuerbach and fashioned on his ideas. In more recent years, there has been an increasing tendency to emphasize special prevention. The judge now has greater discretion in deciding the length of sentences, and he has at his disposal several alternatives to the classical prison sentence. But these changes have not altered the basic character of the system. Unlike mental health acts, penal laws are not designed as prescriptions for people who are in need of treatment because of personality troubles. While there are some exceptions, such as sexual psychopath acts and provisions in penal laws about specific measures to be used when dealing with mentally abnormal people or other special groups of delinquents, penal laws are primarily fashioned to *establish and defend social norms*. As a legislature tries to decide whether to extend or to restrict the area of punishable offenses, or to increase or mitigate the penalty, the focus of attention usually is on the ability of penal laws to modify patterns of behavior. This is the basic question in current debates about the legal treatment of homosexuality, abortion, public prostitution, and drunken driving. From the point of view of sheer logic one must say that general prevention—*i.e.*, assurance that a minimum number of crimes will be committed—must have priority over special prevention—*i.e.*, impeding a particular criminal from future offenses. If general prevention were one hundred percent effective, there would obviously be no need for the imposition of penalties in individual cases.

Ideas about general prevention also have had great effects on the *sentencing policies of courts*. Sometimes this becomes manifest in a dramatic way. In September, 1958, international attention was aroused when the criminal court of Old Bailey sentenced nine young boys, six of them only seventeen years old, to four years of imprisonment for having taken part in race riots involving the use of force against colored people in the Nottinghill district in London.[4] The sentences were considerably heavier than previous sentences in similar cases, and they were meant to be and were regarded as a strong warning to others.[5] Another example occurred in 1945 when the Norwegian Supreme Court sentenced Quisling to death. The first voting judge expressed ideas of general prevention in the following words:

> In a country's hour of fate chaos must not be allowed to reign. And facing the present and the future it must be made clear that a man who, in a critical time in the nation's history, substitutes his own will for the will of constitutional institutions and consequently betrays his country, for him his country has no room.[6]

Ordinarily, there is less drama in the sentencing activities of the courts. The individual decision generally remains within the established tradition of sentencing. But there is no doubt that considerations of general prevention have been important in establishing these patterns. In Norway, the Supreme Court is the court of last resort in matters of sentencing, and it gives reasons for its decisions. General prevention is frequently mentioned. For example, the Supreme Court has established the principle that for reasons of general prevention suspended sentences are not ordinarily imposed in cases involving the use of motor vehicles while in a state of intoxication or in cases involving the use of force against the police.

While general prevention has occupied and still occupies a central position in the philosophy of criminal law, in penal legislation and in the sentencing policies of the courts, it is almost totally neglected in criminology and sociology.[7] It is a deplorable fact that practically no empirical research is being carried out on the subject. In both current criminological debates and the literature of criminology, statements about general prevention are often dogmatic and emotional. They are proclamations of faith which are used as arguments either in favor of or in opposition to the prevailing system. On one hand, we find those who favor authority, severity, and punishment; on the other hand, those who believe in understanding, treatment, and measures of social welfare. The vast majority of criminologists seem to have adopted the second position, and sweeping statements are sometimes put forth as scientific facts. Let me quote a few examples. Barnes and Teeters hold that: "The claim for deterrence is belied by both history and logic. History shows that severe punishments have never reduced criminality to any marked degree."[8] John Ellington has tried to give psychological foundation for the idea: "The belief that punishment protects society from crime by deterring would-be law breakers will not stand up before our new understanding of human behavior."[9] Frequently it is asserted in rather strong terms that the idea of general prevention is merely ancient superstition supported by conservative jurists who have no knowledge whatsoever of human nature. During a debate in 1935, a prominent prison authority in my own country stated:

> With us it is chiefly among the prison authorities and the psychiatrists that we find the supporters of the new ideas

> [*i.e.,* special prevention]. And this is no coincidence, for they study man, while the jurists chiefly read books and files. When a man learns to know and understand criminals he is likely to lose faith in the effectiveness of heavy penalties as a weapon in the war against crime, unless his mental arteries have hardened. He will come to realize that in this struggle entirely different methods produce the actual result.[10]

It is important that empirical questions about the effects of the penal system on the behavior of citizens become detached from ideological arguments so that they can be discussed dispassionately and without bias. As long as no research results are available, legislators and judges necessarily must base their decisions on common sense alone. We should focus on the neglected issue, which is to what degree, and under which conditions, it is possible to direct the behavior of citizens by means of the threat of punishment. This again is part of the more comprehensive problem of determining the extent to which citizens can be guided by means of legal rules.

Some Erroneous Inferences About General Prevention

Certain untenable contentions are frequently introduced in various forms into discussions of general prevention, and it might be helpful to clear them away before we proceed.

1. "Our knowledge of criminals shows us that the criminal law has no deterrent effects."
The fallacy of this argument is obvious. If a man commits a crime, we can only conclude that general prevention has not worked *in his case.* If I interview a thousand prisoners, I collect information about a thousand men in whose cases

general prevention has failed. But I cannot infer from this data that general prevention is ineffective in the cases of all those who have *not* committed crimes. General prevention is more concerned with the psychology of those obedient to the law than with the psychology of criminals.

2. *"The belief in general prevention rests on an untenable rationalistic theory of behavior."*

It is true that the extreme theories of general prevention worked out by people like Bentham and Feuerbach were based on a shallow psychological model in which the actions of men were regarded as the outcome of a rational choice whereby gains and losses were weighed against each other. Similar simplified theories are sometimes expressed by police officials and by authors of letters to newspaper editors asking for heavier penalties. But if we discard such theories, it does not follow that we have to discard the idea of general prevention. Just as fear enters the picture when people take a calculated risk in committing an offense, fear may also be an element in behavior which is not rationally motivated. As mentioned earlier, modern theories of general prevention take into account both deterrence and moral influence, and they concede that the effects involved may be "unconscious and emotional, drawing upon deep rooted fears and aspirations." [11] This does not mean that one's general theory of motivation is of no consequence in assessing the effect of general prevention. The criminologist who believes that a great many people walk about carrying an urge for punishment which may be satisfied by committing crimes is likely to be more skeptical about the value of penal threats than is another who believes that these cases are rare exceptions. Similarly, a man who views human nature optimistically, is less inclined to advocate repressive measures than a person who believes that man is ruthless and egoistic by nature and kept in line only by means of fear.

3. "Legal history shows that general prevention has always been overestimated."

It is true that in the course of history there have been contentions about general prevention which seem fantastic today. There was a time when distinguished members of the House of Lords rose to warn their countrymen that the security of property would be seriously endangered if the administration of justice were weakened by abolition of capital punishment for shoplifting of items having a value of five shillings.[12] Even today, one might find people with exaggerated conceptions of what can be accomplished by means of strong threats of punishment. But the fact that the general-preventive effects of punishment might have been exaggerated does not disprove the existence of such effects.

4. "Because people generally refrain from crimes on moral grounds, threats of penalty have little influence."

The premise contains a large measure of truth, but it does not justify the conclusion. Three comments are necessary. (*A*) Even if people on the whole do not require the criminal law to keep them from committing more serious offenses, this is not true for offenses which are subject to little or no moral reprobation. (*B*) Even though moral inhibitions today are adequate enough to prevent the bulk of the population from committing serious crimes, it is a debatable question whether this would continue for long if the hazards of punishment were removed or drastically minimized. It is conceivable that only a small number of people would fall victim to temptation when the penalties were first abolished or greatly reduced, but that with the passage of time, crime would attract the weaker souls who had become demoralized by seeing offenses committed with impunity. The effects might gradually spread through the population in a chain reaction. (*C*) Even though it be conceded that law abiding conduct in certain areas predominantly depends upon nonlegal conditions, this does not mean that the effects of the legal machinery are not extremely valuable from a community point of view. Let us imagine a fictitious city which has a million adult male inhabitants who commit a hundred rapes annually. Suppose, then, that abolishing the crime of rape led to an increase in the number of rape cases to one thousand. From a social psychological point of view one might conclude that the legal measures were quite insignificant: 999,000 males do not commit rape even when the threat of penalty is absent. If observed from the view point of the legal machinery, however, the conclusion is entirely different. A catastrophic increase of serious cases of violence has occurred. In other words, the increase in rape has demonstrated the tremendous social importance of general prevention.

5. *"To believe in general prevention is to accept brutal penalties."*

This reasoning is apparent in Zilboorg's statement that "if it is true that the punishment of the criminal must have a deterrent effect, then the abolition of the drawing and quartering of criminals was both a logical and penological mistake. Why make punishment milder and thus diminish the deterrent effect of punishment?" [13]

Here we find a mixture of empirical and ethical issues. It was never a principle of criminal justice that crime should be prevented at all costs. Ethical and social considerations will always determine which measures are considered "proper." As Ball has expressed it: "[A] penalty may be quite effective as a deterrent, yet undesirable." [14] Even if it were possible to prove that cutting off thieves' hands would effectively prevent theft, proposals for such practice would scarcely win many adherents today. This paper, however, is primarily concerned with the empirical questions.

SOME BASIC OBSERVATIONS ABOUT
GENERAL PREVENTION

There are other varieties of error about general prevention, but the five types discussed are the basic ones. I shall
now state in greater detail some facts we must bear in mind
when considering general prevention. While most of these
points seem fairly self-evident, they nevertheless are frequently overlooked.

1. *Differences between types of offenses.* The effect of
criminal law on the motivation of individuals is likely to
vary substantially, depending on the character of the norm
being protected. Criminal law theory has for ages distinguished between actions which are immoral in their own
right, *mala per se,* and actions which are illegal merely
because they are prohibited by law, *mala quia prohibita.*
Although the boundaries between these two types of action
are somewhat blurred, the distinction is a fundamental
one. In the case of *mala per se,* the law supports the moral
codes of society. If the threats of legal punishment were
removed, moral feelings and the fear of public judgment
would remain as powerful crime prevention forces, at least
for a limited period. In the case of *mala quia prohibita,*
the law stands alone; conformity is essentially a matter of
effective legal sanctions.

But there are variations within each of these two main
groups. Let us take the ban on incest and the prohibition
of theft, as examples. As a moral matter, the prohibition of
incest is nearly universal, but violations are not legally
punishable everywhere. I doubt that the absence of a threat
of punishment seriously influences the number of cases of
incest. The moral prohibition of incest is so closely inte-
grated with family structure that there is little need for
the support of the criminal law. Stealing, however, is an
entirely different matter. As Leslie Wilkins puts it: "The

average normal housewife does not need to be deterred from poisoning her husband, but possibly does need a deterrent from shoplifting." [15] And what applies to stealing applies even more to tax dodging. In this field, experience seems to show that the majority of citizens are potential criminals. Generally speaking, the more rational and normally motivated a specific violation may appear, the greater the importance of criminal sanctions as a means of sustaining lawfulness.

Any realistic discussion of general prevention must be based on a distinction between various types of norms and on an analysis of the circumstances motivating transgression in each particular type.[16] This is a fact easily overlooked, and authors often discuss general prevention as if all norms were the same. Probably they have certain basic types of offenses in mind—for instance murder or property violations—but they fail to make this limitation explicit.

2. *Differences between persons.* Citizens are not equally receptive to the general-preventive effects of the penal system. The intellectual prerequisites to understanding and assessing the threat of punishment may be deficient or totally absent. Children, the insane, and those suffering from mental deficiency are, for this reason, poor objects of general prevention. In other cases, the emotional preconditions are missing; some people more than others are slaves of the desires and impulses of the moment, even when realizing that they may have to pay dearly for their self-indulgence. In addition, psychiatrists claim that some people have feelings of guilt and consequent cravings for penance that lead them to commit crimes for the purpose of bringing punishment upon themselves.

Just as intellectual and emotional defects reduce the deterrent effects of punishment, they may also render an individual more or less unsusceptible to the moral influences of the law. While most members of the community will normally be inclined to accept the provisions and prohibitions of the law, this attitude is not uniform. Some people exhibit extreme opposition to authority either in the form of indifference or overaggression and defiance.

3. *Differences between societies.* The criminal laws do not operate in a cultural vacuum. Their functions and importance vary radically according to the kind of society which they serve. In a small, slowly changing community the informal social pressures are strong enough to stimulate a large measure of conformity without the aid of penal laws. In an expanding urbanized society with a large degree of mobility this social control is weakened, and the mechanisms of legal control assume a far more basic role.[17]

Even in countries which have reached equivalent stages of economic development, the cultural atmosphere may differ. After a visit to the United States in the 1930's, two leading European criminologists found that the American attitude toward the law was different from the attitude in the more tradition bound European societies. The Austrian criminologist Grassberger spoke of the lack of a legal conscience (*Rechtsbewusstsein*) in the European sense.[18] The Swedish psychiatrist Kinberg emphasized

> the apparently slight influence exercised by the penal laws on the public opinion of morals. The legislative mill grinds as it does in European countries, but the average American cares little what comes out of it. His own behavior-patterns are but slightly affected by the fact that the penal law disapproves of a certain behavior-pattern, but so much the more by the opinion of his own social group, *i.e.,* the people with whom his psychological relations are more or less personal, *e.g.,* his family, friends, fellow workers, acquaintances, clubs, etc.[19]

4. *Conflicting group norms.* The motivating influences of the penal law may become more or less neutralized by group norms working in the opposite direction. The group may be a religious organization which opposes compulsory military service, or it may be a criminal gang acting

for the sake of profit. It may be organized labor fighting against strike legislation which they regard as unjust, or it may be a prohibited political party that wants to reform the entire social and political order of the day. It may be a subjugated minority using every means available in its struggle for equality, or the dominating group of society which employs every means available to prevent the minority from enjoying in practice the equality it is promised in law. Or perhaps it may be an ethnic or social group whose traditional patterns of living clash with the laws of society.

In such cases, the result is a conflict between the formalized community laws, which are expressed through the criminal law, and the counteracting norms dominating the group. Against the moral effects of the penal law stands the moral influence of the group; against the fear of legal sanction stands the fear of group sanction, which may range from the loss of social status to economic boycott, violence, and even homicide.

5. *Law obedience in law enforcement agencies.* The question of general prevention is normally treated as a matter of the private citizen's obedience of the law. However, a similar question may be raised about law enforcement agencies. All countries have outlawed corruption and neglect of duty within the police and the civil service, but in many places they are serious problems. In all probability, there are few areas in which the crime rates differ so much from country to country. Laxity and corruption in law enforcement in its turn is bound to reduce the general-preventive effects of criminal law.

Variations in General Prevention With Changes in Legislation and Enforcement

It is a matter of basic interest, from a practical point of view, to determine how general prevention varies according to changes in legislation or legal machinery. Such changes may be classified into four different categories.

1. *The risk of detection, apprehension and conviction.* The efficiency of the system could be changed, for example, by intensifying or reducing the effort of the police or by altering the rules of criminal procedure so as to increase or lower the probabilities that criminals will escape punishment. Even the simplest kind of common sense indicates that the degree of risk of detection and conviction is of paramount importance to the preventive effects of the penal law. Very few people would violate the law if there were a policeman on every doorstep. It has even been suggested that the insanity of an offender be determined by asking whether he would have performed the prohibited act "with a policeman at his elbow." [20]

Exceptions would occur, however. Some crimes are committed in such a state of excitement that the criminal acts without regard to the consequences. In other cases the actor accepts the penalty as a reasonable price for carrying out the action—we may think of the attitude a busy salesman has toward parking regulations. Further, a political assassin may deliberately sacrifice his life to his cause. But there is good reason to believe that certainty of rapid apprehension and punishment would prevent *most* violations.[21]

On the other hand, there is evidence that the lack of enforcement of penal laws designed to regulate behavior in morally neutral fields may rapidly lead to mass infringements. Parking regulations, currency regulations, and price regulations are examples of such laws.[22] The individual's moral reluctance to break the law is not strong enough to secure obedience when the law comes into conflict with his personal interests.

There is an interesting interplay between moral reprobation and legal implementation. At least three conditions combine to prevent an individual from perpetrating a punishable act he is tempted to perform: his moral inhibitions, his fear of the censure of his associates, and his fear of punishment. The latter two elements are interwoven in many ways. A law violation may become known to the criminal's family, friends, and neighbors even if there is no arrest or prosecution. However, it is frequently the process of arrest, prosecution, and trial which brings the affair into the open and exposes the criminal to the censure of his associates. If the criminal can be sure that there will be no police action, he can generally rest assured that there will be no social reprobation. The legal machinery, therefore, is in itself the most effective means of mobilizing that kind of social control which emanates from community condemnation.

Reports on conditions of disorganization following wars, revolutions, or mutinies provide ample documentation as to how lawlessness may flourish when the probability of detection, apprehension, and conviction is low.[23] In these situations, however, many factors work together. The most clear-cut examples of the importance of the risk of detection itself are provided by cases in which society functions normally but all policing activity is paralyzed by a police strike or a similar condition. For example, the following official report was made on lawlessness during a 1919 police strike, starting at midnight on July 31, during which nearly half of the Liverpool policemen were out of service:

> In this district the strike was accompanied by threats, violence and intimidation on the part of lawless persons. Many assaults on the constables who remained on duty were committed. Owing to the sudden nature of the strike the authorities were afforded no opportunity to make adequate provision to cope with the position. Looting of shops commenced about 10 P.M. on August 1st, and continued for some days. In all about 400 shops were looted.

Military were requisitioned, special constables sworn in, and police brought from other centers.[24]

A somewhat similar situation occurred in Denmark when the German occupation forces arrested the entire police force in September, 1944. During the remainder of the occupation period all policing was performed by an improvised unarmed watch corps, who were ineffective except in those instances when they were able to capture the criminal red-handed. The general crime rate rose immediately, but there was a great discrepancy between the various types of crime.[25] The number of cases of robbery increased generally in Copenhagen during the war, rising from ten per year in 1939 to ten per month in 1943. But after the Germans arrested the police in 1944, the figure rose to over a hundred per month and continued to rise. Larcenies reported to the insurance companies quickly increased tenfold and more. The fact that penalties were greatly increased for criminals who were caught and brought before the courts did not offset the fact that most crimes were going undetected. On the other hand, crimes like embezzlement and fraud, where the criminal is usually known if the crime itself is discovered, do not seem to have increased notably.

Unfortunately, none of these reports tells us whether the rise in criminality was due to increased activity among established criminals or whether noncriminals participated as well. Kinberg, basing his observations on studies of the French Revolution and other political upheavals, holds that the rate increases primarily because existing criminal and asocial elements take advantage of the unusual circumstances, but that men who were "potential criminals" before the crisis also make a contribution.

The involuntary experiments in Liverpool and Copenhagen showed a reduction in law obedience following a reduction of risks. Examples of the opposite are also reported—the number of crimes decreases as the hazards rise. Tarde mentions that the number of cases of poisoning decreased when research in chemistry and toxicology made it possible to discover with greater certainty the causes as well as the perpetrator of this type of crime.[26] A decline in bank robberies and kidnappings in the United States is reported to have followed the enactment of federal legislation which increased the likelihood of punishment.[27]

A Swedish postwar experience is also worth noting. In order to save gasoline during the Suez crisis of 1956, Sweden prohibited the driving of private automobiles on weekends. While special permission to drive could be obtained (the necessary permit had to be affixed to the windshield of the car), most cars were immobilized. This prohibition, of course, greatly increased the risks involved in stealing cars on weekends. A considerable decrease in the number of automobile thefts is said to have occurred on Saturdays and Sundays during the period of prohibition, especially in the larger cities.[28] It appears that even such a youthful and unstable group as the automobile thieves in the Scandinavian countries—mostly "joyriders"—reacts to an increased risk when the increase is tangible enough.

The decisive factor in creating the deterrent effect is, of course, not the objective risk of detection but the risk as it is calculated by the potential criminal. We know little about how realistic these calculations are. It is often said that criminals tend to be overly optimistic—they are confident that all will work out well. It is possible that the reverse occurs among many law abiding people; they are deterred because of an over-estimation of the risks. A faulty estimate in one direction or the other may consequently play an important part in determining whether an individual is to become a criminal. If fluctuations in the risks of detection do not reach the potential offender, they can be of no consequence to deterrence. If, on the other hand, it were possible to convince people that crime does not pay, this assumption might act as a deterrent even if the risks, viewed objectively, remained unchanged.

Popular notions regarding the risks of convictions are also likely to have a bearing on the moral effects of the criminal law. The law's moral influence on the citizen is likely to be weakened if the law can be violated with impunity. The law abiding citizen who has subdued his antisocial inclinations might become frustrated when he observes others follow their desires without experiencing disagreeable consequences. He will not be able to confirm that his sacrifice was worthwhile.[29] Violations unknown to him, of course, will not produce similar results.

However, for some types of crime even an occasional enforcement of the law may bring about considerable preventive effects. Criminal abortion convictions in most countries seem very rare in relation to the real crime rate. In Norway, a Public Law Committee in 1956 estimated that the annual number of illegal abortions was approximately 7,000.[30] During the preceding five years, on the average only twenty persons a year were found guilty of this offense. The situation in many other countries is much the same.[31] In spite of such infrequent law enforcement, however, most people who have given attention to the problem are convinced that a removal of the penal threat will lead to a decisive rise in the number of abortions. I do not believe that the threat of punishment has much deterrent effect on the women who desire abortion, but it makes it more difficult for them to find a doctor (or a quack) willing to perform the operation; moreover, the legal prohibition may influence the general attitude toward abortion. The Soviet experiment lends support to this position. To counteract quack abortions, the doors of the state hospitals were opened in 1920 for free interruptions of pregnancy. By 1930, the number of registered abortions in Leningrad and Moscow was one and one-half times as high as the number of births and still quack abor-

tions had not disappeared.[32] In other countries of Eastern
Europe and in Japan, the legalization or liberalization of
abortion after World War II has been followed by an
enormous rise in the number of abortions.[33]

2. *The severity of penalties.* At least since the time of
Beccaria, it has been commonly accepted that the certainty
of detection and punishment is of greater consequence in
deterring people from committing crimes than is the severity of the penalty. This notion has undoubtedly contributed significantly to the abolition of brutal penalties,
and there is certainly a large measure of truth in it. Part
of the explanation is that one who ponders the possibility
of detection and punishment before committing a crime
must necessarily consider the total social consequences, of
which the penalty is but a part. A trusted cashier committing embezzlement, a minister who evades payment of his
taxes, a teacher making sexual advances towards minors,
and a civil servant who accepts bribes have a fear of detection which is more closely linked with the dread of public scandal and subsequent social ruin than with appre-
hensions of legal punishment. Whether the punishment
is severe or mild thus appears to be rather unimportant.
However, in cases of habitual criminals or juvenile delinquents from the slums the situation may be quite different.

Even if we accept Beccaria's position, it does not follow that the severity of penalties is without importance.
It is difficult to increase the likelihood of detection and
punishment because the risk of detection usually depends
on many conditions beyond the reach of the authorities,
and because improvement of police effectiveness requires
money and human resources. Accordingly, when the legislators and courts attempt to check any apparent rise in the
crime rate they generally increase the severity of penalties.
On the other hand, for those who wish to make the crimi-

nal law more humane the problem is one of determining how far it is possible to proceed in the direction of leniency without weakening the law's total preventive effects. It is impossible to avoid the question of how important a change in the severity of the punishment may be under standard conditions of detection, apprehension, and conviction. For the judge this is the only form in which the problem presents itself.

A potential criminal who reflects upon the possibilities of punishment may pay attention to the severity of the penalty to which he exposes himself, as well as to the risk of detection. He may be willing to run the risk of a year's imprisonment but he might not gamble ten. The situation is similar to those in which nature herself attaches penalties to certain actions. Sexual promiscuity has always brought with it the risk of undesired children and of venereal diseases, and consideration of these risks has certainly in the course of time persuaded many people to exercise self-restraint. The progress of civilization has led to a diminishing of the former risk and rendered the latter less formidable. Few people will deny that these changes have had a considerable bearing on the development of sexual mores in the Western world.

One weakness in the mechanism of deterrence is the fact that threats of future punishment, especially if apprehension is uncertain, do not have the same motivating power as the desires of the moment. While some people live in a state of perpetual anxiety and concern for the future, others focus only on the present. There have always been people who have been willing to risk eternal pain as the price of satisfying worldly desires in this life. Moreover, when the risks of detection are considered small, it is possible that questions about the severity of the penalty tend to lose their significance. As we indicated earlier, the criminal often acts upon the assumption that all is going to end well; what might take place if he is caught is pushed into the background. It is also possible, of course, that the very severity of the penalty—the magnitude of the risk—may give the illegal action a special appeal, in the way that dangerous sports are attractive to some people.

Other factors may also enter the picture. A professional criminal may be so strongly involved in his profession that he feels there are no real alternatives regardless of the penalties. The newspapers recently reported the activities of an eighty-seven-year-old Greek pick-pocket who was once more facing the court. He had fifty previous convictions, and had spent some fifty years behind prison walls in Greece or abroad. He was released from prison by amnesty on the occasion of King Constantine's wedding, but a few weeks later he was caught in the act of taking money from a man in an elevator. In the face of such a set pattern of life, the threat of punishment is simply ineffective.

Even more complicated than the connection between the magnitude of the penalty and its deterrent effect is the connection between the magnitude of the penalty and its moral effect. Heavy penalties are an expression of strong social condemnation, and prima facie one might assume that the heavier the penalty the greater its moral effect. However, it is not that simple. In fact, we are concerned here with two problems. One problem is that of determining the impact of stronger or lesser severity of the *entire penal system*. In the Scandinavian countries, sentences are on the whole much more lenient than in the United States. A penalty of three years imprisonment in Norway marks the crime as very grave, quite unlike the situation in the United States. Perhaps what takes place is an adjustment between the penalties employed and their evaluation by the public, so that social disapproval may be both expressed and graded almost as efficiently by means of lenient sentences as by severe ones. The second problem is that of determining the impact of stronger or milder penalties for *certain types of offenses*. Is it possible to use legislation and court practice as devices to influence where, on their scale of condemnation, citizens are to place different types of violations? Stephen seemed to have extreme confidence in the power of legislation when he said: "The sentence of the law is to the moral sentiment of the public in relation to any offence what a seal is to hot wax." [34] But it might be maintained with equal justification that while the law certainly serves to strengthen the moral inhibitions against crime in general, it is not very successful in pressing upon the public its own evaluation of various types of conduct. Experience, at least, seems to show that old laws which run counter to new ideas have a tendency to fade out of use and, eventually, to be repealed. A recent paper by Walker and Argyle gives some support to the notion that mere knowledge that a form of conduct is a criminal offense has little bearing on the moral attitude of individuals toward that conduct.[35]

Questions about the importance of punishment have been discussed in great detail with reference to whether capital punishment for murder is conducive to greater preventive effects than life imprisonment. Comparisons between states employing capital punishment and states which have abolished it, as well as comparisons of the frequency of murder before and after abolition, reveal no stable correlations and have led most criminologists to conclude that capital punishment is of little or no consequence. The lack of correlation is understandable from a psychological point of view. In the first place, murder in our culture is surrounded by massive moral reprobation. Accordingly, the inhibitions against murder usually are broken only in situations of emotional excitement or intense pressure in which the criminal disregards the consequences. Secondly, if the potential criminal deliberates about the risk of punishment before he takes action, then both the death penalty and life imprisonment will appear so drastic that the difference between them may seem fairly insignificant. He relies on going undetected; if he is detected, he has lost.

The moral effects of capital punishment also must be considered. It may be said that capital punishment for murder exerts a moral influence by indicating that life is the most highly protected value. Perhaps this is what Stephen was expressing in his famous words: "Some men, probably, abstain from murder because they fear that, if they committed murder, they would be hung. Hundreds of thousands abstain from it because they regard it with horror. One great reason why they regard it with horror is, that murderers are hung with the hearty approbation of all reasonable men." [36] But it is worth noting that we find here a discrepancy between aims and means which is likely to weaken the moral effect of capital punishment. The law attempts to impress upon society a respect for human life as an absolute value while, at the same time, this respect is disregarded by employing the death penalty to punish the offender.

It would, however, be incorrect to conclude, on the basis of existing evidence, that the death penalty is always ineffective. In his book on terrorism and communism, Trotsky points out that after a revolution the deposed party fighting to regain power cannot become frightened by threats of imprisonment because no one believes in the permanence of the new regime. The death penalty by contrast retains its deterrent effect—"the revolution kills a few and intimidates the thousands." [37] Experiences in my own country during the German occupation in the Second World War give rise to similar observations. To work against the occupants was considered by the great majority of the people to be morally just. To be arrested for illegal activities therefore brought about no loss of social esteem. On the contrary, the victims of the Gestapo were regarded by the population with affection and admiration. During the last part of the war, when the population counted the continuation of the occupation by months or weeks, even the threat of life imprisonment meant no more than the risk of transitory detention. In such a context, the threat of capital punishment produced a thoroughly different and more frightening effect than the notion of arrest and imprisonment. Experience during the occupation of Norway also shows how the risk of punishment might produce different results according to the national attitude of the individual and his receptiveness to danger. A large share of the population wanted to run no risks. Although sympathetic to the resistance movement, it would not become involved. Another large share of the public was willing to take part in resistance activities as long as the dangers were limited and their lives would not be in peril. Members of a third group would not allow themselves to be intimidated by notions of either death or torture.

It is unfortunate that discussions of general prevention have concentrated on the effects of capital punishment for murder. In most societies, murder is a rare crime which attracts a disproportionate amount of attention. At least in the Scandinavian countries, the victims of murder are very few in comparison with the victims of careless automobile driving, but for emotional reasons murder is more interesting than traffic deaths. Even in an emotional crime like murder, with all its pathological elements, it would be untenable to claim that the magnitude of the punishment has no effect whatsoever. If punishment of three or four years' imprisonment became the standard sentence for murder, the risk connected with murder done for the sake of profit would diminish and this kind of crime would probably increase. In the long run, such a reduction in penalty might also reduce the inhibitions against committing murder in situations where murder seems a tempting escape from a situation of emotional conflict.

Interesting lessons may be drawn from an experiment

launched in some of the Scandinavian countries to fight drunken driving. In Norway, for example, the motor vehicle code prohibits driving of motor vehicles when the alcohol percentage in the driver's blood exceeds 0.05,[38] a percentage which in clinical examinations would rarely produce behavioral changes significant enough to allow the drawing of uncontestable conclusions about a state of drunkenness or intoxication. A driver who is suspected of violating the provision must consent to a blood test, and it is not necessary to prove that the driver was unfit to drive because of his consumption of alcohol, so there is only very rarely any question of proof. And the consistent policy of the courts has been to give prison sentences for violations, except in cases involving very exceptional circumstances. The prison terms are short, usually not much more than the minimum jail period of twenty-one days, but the penalty is exacted on anyone who is detected, whether or not the driving was dangerous or caused damage.

A person moving between Norway and the United States can hardly avoid noticing the radical difference in the attitudes towards automobile driving and alcohol. There is no reason to doubt that the difference in legal provisions plays a substantial role in this difference in attitudes. The awareness of hazards of imprisonment for intoxicated driving is in our country a living reality to every driver, and for most people the risk seems too great. When a man goes to a party where alcoholic drinks are likely to be served, and if he is not fortunate enough to have a wife who drives but does not drink, he will leave his car at home or he will limit his consumption to a minimum. It is also my feeling—although I am here on uncertain grounds—that the legislation has been instrumental in forming or sustaining the widespread conviction that it is wrong, or irresponsible, to place oneself behind the wheel when intoxicated. "Alcohol and motor car driving do not belong together" is a slogan commonly accepted. Statistics on traffic accidents show a very small number of accidents due to intoxication.[39]

It should not be concluded that there is anything like absolute obedience to the laws regulating drunken driving. Every year a considerable number of people are convicted for violations, and the number has risen in proportion to the increase in the number of automobiles. In recent years, more persons have been sentenced to imprisonment for this misdemeanor than for all felonies put together. And there are, of course, a large number of citizens whose violations of the law go undetected because neither their management of the car nor their general behavior arouses suspicion. Interviews with students have revealed considerable hidden criminality even in this field. But the fact that violations occur does not interfere with our conclusion that the severity of the legislation has to a very high degree limited the incidence of driving after drinking.

It seems reasonable to conclude that as a general rule, though not without exceptions, the general-preventive effect of the criminal law increases with the growing severity of penalties. Contemporary dictatorships display with almost frightening clarity the conformity that can be produced by a ruthlessly severe justice.

However, it is necessary to make two important reservations. In the first place, as we indicated when discussing the risk of detection, what is decisive is not the actual practice but how this practice is conceived by the public. Although little research has been done to find out how much the general public knows about the penal system, presumably most people have only vague and unspecified notions. Therefore, only quite substantial changes will be noticed. Only rarely does a single sentence bring about significant preventive effects.

In the second place, the prerequisite of general prevention is that the law be enforced. Experience seems to show that excessively severe penalties may actually reduce the risk of conviction, thereby leading to results contrary to their purpose. When the penalties are not reasonably attuned to the gravity of the violation, the public is less inclined to inform the police, the prosecuting authorities are less disposed to prosecute and juries are less apt to convict. Beutel has provided an excellent illustration of this in his study of the severe bad check laws in Nebraska. He concludes his examination of the policy of county attorneys and sheriffs as follows: "In all, the Nebraska picture is one of spotty performance by law enforcement officials, varying all the way from those who are frustrated by the enormity of enforcing the laws as written and consequently do nothing or as little as possible to those who try to enforce the statute literally but usually fail at re-election." [40] By comparison, he found that bad checks were rarer in Colorado, where the law was milder but enforcement was more uniform and effective.[41]

3. *Punishment or treatment.* There is ample reason to believe that the general-preventive effects of punishment are connected with the main features of the penal system. For example, minor revisions of the rules about mitigating or aggravating circumstances in the meting out of punishment cannot easily be imagined as having demonstrable effects as long as fundamental changes in the direction of mitigation or aggravation are not being introduced. From a practical point of view this means that considerations of individual prevention could be taken into account to a considerable degree without noticeably impairing the general-preventive effects.

But it may well be asked what would happen if the existing penal system were abolished in favor of a purely treatment oriented system. This approach would be similar to the method currently used for children, the insane and mentally defective—incarceration is employed only to the extent deemed necessary in view of the problems of particular individuals, and any loss of liberty accompanying the incarceration is not intended as punishment.

To begin with, it is evident that even measures which are "pure treatment" may convey a deterrent influence similar to that of regular punishment. For example, a treatment program aimed at remodeling the criminal's personality and norm system often presupposes institutional treatment over a longer period than is necessary if the criminal is merely being punished. But from the point of view of general prevention the problem lies at the other end of the scale—in cases where the individual offender requires little or no treatment. This relates to one aspect of the problem which we touched on previously, namely how far it is possible to proceed in the direction of leniency without significantly reducing the preventive effects of the criminal law.[42]

It is hardly worthwhile to proceed further into discussions of the relationships of treatment and general prevention at this time. It is difficult to imagine what a purely treatment system might be. We know as yet very little about what kinds of treatment are most suitable for what kinds of criminals and even less about how, or whether, the rate of success varies according to the duration and intensity. Systems based on the treatment ideology could conceivably take forms which are utterly dissimilar from the point of view of general prevention. What appears realistic today is the application of treatment programs to limited categories of criminals. Discussions of treatment and general prevention must therefore take place in connection with such limited problems. For many categories of offenses a system of treatment does not seem to be at all a real alternative to the existing repressive system. Such offenses are, for example, espionage, careless driving, tax dodging, corruption among civil servants, violations of laws involving economic regulation, and all those similar prescriptions of order characterizing modern societies. In such cases, it is apparent to even the strongest believers in a treatment ideology that the basic function of the intervention of society is to create respect for social norms, not to cure individuals of their asocial inclinations.

4. *Restriction or expansion of the penal system.* It may be interesting to speculate on what effects would occur if the entire penal system—the criminal law, the police, the courts, the prisons—were removed and no other apparatus of legal sanction substituted for it. According to Marxist ideology, this condition will be attained when the final Communist society has been established. The theory assumes that everyone will perform his duty willingly and habitually so that it will not be necessary to use punishment or other means of coercion, and consequently the state will wither away. But as we look at the actual developments within Communist countries we see no obvious signs that the state is withering away or that the police or punishment have been eliminated. Nearly half a century after the Russian Revolution, we find capital punishment used in the Soviet Union not only for treason but for economic crimes as well.

There may be fields where a sufficient degree of conformity could be reached without any sanction, by appealing to the citizens and making it easy for them to conform. But it does not seem probable that such techniques will be widely applicable. If it is felt necessary to interfere through legislation, it will normally also be felt necessary to put a sanction behind the rules. A threat of punishment is the traditional means of enforcement. Perhaps greater imagination should be used to develop alternatives to punishment.

It seems fairly safe to predict that no society will experiment in these matters to the extent of abolishing the basic penal provisions protecting life, bodily safety, or property. The involuntary experiments created by police strikes or similar conditions support the notion that a highly urbanized industrial society can scarcely exist without police and criminal courts or a state power apparatus with similar functions. However, outside the basic areas protected by the criminal law the direction is much less certain. The regulation of economic activities through the use of criminal sanctions has varied from country to country. Religious offenses constitute another field in which there have been great fluctuations in the penal approach. Similarly, there currently is a great degree of uncertainty concerning the legal treatment of many activities rooted in or related to sex, such as prostitution, homosexuality, *crimen bestialitatis,* and pornography. Abortion constitutes still another category which is subject to differing legal evaluations. Political crimes also deserve to be mentioned. In some countries there is nearly boundless freedom for verbal attacks on the government and the prevailing social order, while in others any kind of criticism is considered a dangerous crime against the state.

Just an enumeration of some of these categories of crimes conveys the hopelessness of treating them as a single unit. Any discussion of the possibility—and desirability —of making citizens conform by means of the penal law must treat each category separately, and it must be based on detailed information about the activity being discussed. "Motivation" and "detection risks" are necessary key words in such a discussion. Prohibition laws in the United States and in some European countries after World War I are horrendous examples of miscalculation on the part of legislators. The experiments illustrate how difficult it is to evoke respect for penal provisions regarded by the bulk of the population as an undue interference with their freedom.

RESEARCH POSSIBILITIES ON THE EFFICACY
OF GENERAL PREVENTION

When for practical reasons it is necessary to estimate the general-preventive effects of some specific alternative as opposed to another, the estimate is usually made by means of common psychological reasoning. For example, on the basis of rather cloudy notions of human nature and social conditions, law committees and judges sometimes try to predict how a certain innovation is likely to function in a particular situation in a given society. The more realistic the psychology applied, and the more thorough the knowledge about the activity concerned, the more probable it is that an estimate is somewhere near the truth.

It is now fashionable to hold that we have no knowledge whatever about general prevention. As should be apparent from the preceding material, I believe this to be a considerable exaggeration. In fact, it may well be maintained that we have more knowledge, at least more useful knowledge, about the general-preventive effects of punishment than about special-preventive effects. A generation ago, prison authorities and psychiatrists believed they knew a good deal about how to treat criminals. Recent research, especially that conducted in England and California on the comparative effects of various sanctions, seems to show that, on the whole, these notions were illusions.[43] This research suggests that there is little difference between the overall results of various kinds of treatment when consideration is given to differences in the composition of the population being treated. Probation shows almost the same results as institutional treatment; a short period of treatment about the same results as a long one; traditional disciplinary institutional treatment on the whole appears to have results similar to those produced by treatment in modern, therapeutically-oriented institutions.

It may be that overall success rates are improper measures of the effects of different treatments, because one type of treatment may be effective with one type of offender and not with another. The attempts to work out a typology with which to verify such an hypothesis have not gone beyond the "pilot study" stage. The present state of knowledge does not provide adequate grounds for erecting a penal system based on special preventive points of view.

Continuing research on treatment is necessary. No less important, however, is research designed to shed more light on questions of general prevention. From time to time it is held that there is no scientific method of research into general prevention. This, in my opinion, is unwarranted defeatism. The problems are difficult, especially in relation to the long range moral effects of the criminal law, but scarcely more difficult than many other problems dealt with in sociological or social psychological research. Let us examine the methods at our disposal.

1. *Comparisons between geographic areas.* This method has been employed in discussions of the effects of capital punishment. Areas using the death penalty for murder are compared to areas where there is no death penalty for this crime, with a view to determining whether there is any connection between the punishment and the murder rates. The method certainly has its difficulties. Statistics show only the criminality which has been detected, and it is difficult to obtain full knowledge of the factors which may influence the ratio of undetected crime. Even if the comparative method reveals a real difference in the extent of criminality, we still must judge whether the difference is due to the penal system or to other social conditions. In order to draw definite conclusions we need areas with similar social conditions but drastic differences in legal systems, and such areas are difficult to find. Systems of penal sanctions are usually quite similar in countries

which are close to each other in the fields of economic and cultural development. If certain behavior is punishable in one country but not in another, we may face an additional difficulty arising from the fact that in the second country the behavior not regarded as criminal will ordinarily not be investigated or registered.

In certain areas, however, there is hope for fruitful comparisons. By and large, these are fields where sources other than police or court statistics can be utilized to measure the occurrence of a specific type of deviance. Abortion was mentioned previously as a field in which comparisons between differing areas may be both possible and valuable. Beutel compared the operation of Nebraska's bad check laws with the operation of similar laws in Colorado, Vermont, and New Hampshire.[44] Information about the number and extent of bad checks was supplied by banks, and information about financial losses for bad checks in various types of businesses was obtained by means of questionnaires.

Intoxication among drivers is another field in which it should be possible to carry out sound geographic comparisons. In this field we find great divergences concerning legislation and legal practice. At the same time, the effects of legislation could be studied by using a variety of techniques, for example, by conducting alcohol tests of randomly selected motor car drivers, by interviews or by means of alcohol tests on deceased traffic victims. Many practical and methodological difficulties must be overcome, but I am confident that by expending a reasonable amount of labor and money it will be possible to reach results of great relevance to the solution of a serious social problem in the motor age.

2. *Comparisons in time*. When revisions are made in penal provisions, in the organization of the police, and in the practice of the prosecuting authorities or of the courts,

the extent of criminality can be examined with a view to assessing the changes. The difficulties here are similar to those encountered when making geographical comparisons. Radical and sudden changes in legal systems and the machinery of justice are rare. As a rule, change takes place through gradual alterations, for example, in the direction of stronger or milder penalties or in the degree of police effectiveness. As these alterations occur, there are changes in other fields bearing upon criminality, and it is extremely difficult to isolate each factor in order to determine what produced the final result. Changes introduced into the system may further influence the registration of crimes, so that the statistics are not comparable.[45] This difficulty is compounded when new penal provisions are introduced or old ones abolished, because generally only violations are recorded—we do not keep records of nonconformity before it becomes a crime or after it ceases to be a crime. Such statistical problems may, however, be overcome in areas where there are objective data on the extent of the nonconformity.

Drastic changes in law enforcement often take place during wars or revolutions, but so many other conditions change simultaneously that it is difficult to draw valid conclusions which apply to normal conditions. The most advantageous basis for conclusions about causal connections is found when great and sudden changes take place in law enforcement while the life of the community proceeds in its normal groove. The police strike, from the point of view of the social scientist, is an ideal situation, but unfortunately for the scientist, society does not permit the strike to continue long enough for exhaustive study.

In spite of the difficulties involved, the method of comparisons in time should not be underestimated. Most of what we know about general prevention comes from what history can tell us. Tarde presented a vast amount of material from various countries and periods,[46] while Kinberg concentrated on revolutions and similar conditions.[47] Radzinowicz has provided much material on the importance of a well-organized and effective police.[48] I am sure that a great deal more could become known through systematic exploitation of historical materials. Unfortunately, criminologists ordinarily are not historians, and historians are rarely inclined to concentrate on problems of general prevention.

Even better than to study the past is to watch the changes as they are taking place. This method was employed by Moore and Callahan in their well-known study of public reactions to changes in parking regulations, a study more remarkable for its methods and its theoretical basis than for its results.[49] Just as new types of penal institutions should not be introduced unless opportunities are provided for research on the effects of the new measures, important changes in the law or in legal practice should always be correlated with a program of research designed to examine the effects on crime as a whole. The research does not have to be limited to the public legal machinery. Large enterprises producing or marketing easily and widely consumed goods such as tobacco and alcohol have the everlasting problem of preventing theft among their own employees. They have their own system of controls and their own means of sanction. Perhaps research in this area will shed light on how the ordinary citizen resists the temptation to steal and also will show how employees react to changes in risks when control measures are introduced. Studies of the use of lie detector tests in American business enterprises have indicated widespread dishonesty even among those who are ordinarily held above suspicion, and they also have shown that such tests have a deterrent value upon the future conduct of employees.[50]

3. *Experiments.* Any change of a legal provision or a policy of the police, prosecuting authorities, or the courts

is, in a way, an experiment. Although such alterations are primarily made to gain certain effects, not to increase our knowledge, to a certain degree they may be made with a view to research. Moore and Callahan's study of parking included experiments conducted in concert with the police authorities. Another experiment recently initiated in Finland attempts to appraise the deterring effect of fines imposed for drunkenness.[51] The local police of three middle-sized towns have agreed to reduce heavily the percentage of prosecutions for persons arrested for drunkenness. The results of the experiment are to be measured principally by comparing the number of arrests for drunkenness before and after the change. Other towns, especially three towns with approximately the same number of inhabitants and the same number of arrests for drunkenness as the three experiment towns, are to be used as controls. The results of the experiment are not yet available. It seems doubtful, however, that the difference in stimuli in this experiment is sufficiently great to produce conclusive results.

It seems realistic to assume that legal, administrative, and economic considerations will impose rather narrow limits for purely research-motivated experiments. It is more economical to await alterations which are made for other than experimental reasons and to use the opportunity to promote optimal research conditions with a view to recording the effects.

4. *Research on motivation, communication, and personality development.* The kind of research I have been discussing is socio-statistical. It aims at uncovering connections between changes in the function of the legal apparatus and changes in criminality. Even where such connections have been discovered, nothing has been directly revealed about the psychological mechanisms at work, and it is therefore difficult to generalize about the results. Accordingly, research must also probe the individual links in

the theories of general prevention. Instead of trying to give direct answers to questions about the effect of the penal law on behavior, one may break the main problem into partial problems accessible to research. Perhaps Aubert is right when he contends that "the problem of general prevention constitutes a huge mosaic. The bulk of the stones constituting it must be obtained from general sociology and social psychology." [52]

Thus far in this article I have touched on a good many empirical questions to which we do not know the answers. How widespread and detailed is popular knowledge about legal norms? What are the attitudes toward the legal machinery, and how common is aggression or indifference as opposed to positive support? What proportion of the population has the feelings of guilt and the urge for punishment so often referred to by psychoanalysts? To what extent do criminals think of the risks when they plan or perform a punishable act, and how realistic is their estimate of the risks? How do people at large react to risks? These are questions which focus on the problems already discussed. In addition there are questions related to communication theory. How is knowledge about legislation and the legal machinery transmitted? What is the role of mass media as compared to personal contacts, and what connections exist between the forms of information and their motivating power?

We may also ask how the threat of punishment influences the psychological processes of potential criminals. The following two-step hypothesis has been put forward. A person refraining from a desired action because of a penal threat will experience dissonance. Since an effective way of reducing dissonance is by derogating the action, he will then convince himself that he really did not want to do it. In testing this hypothesis, it is essential to determine the manner and degree to which the process depends on the severity of the punishment.[53]

We may also analyze the development and internalization of moral conceptions by individuals. What is the influence of police, punishment, and prison in the socialization process? To what extent does the penal law indirectly influence child rearing practices by instilling in parents a desire to prevent their children from coming into conflict with the law and the legal machinery? What defensive mechanisms may be utilized by the criminal to convince himself that his violation is not really a criminal act? What are the psychological effects on the law-abiding citizen when he sees crimes committed with impunity? Surely psychologists and sociologists can formulate such questions in a manner that makes them answerable by empirical research and in a manner that attunes them to research already completed.

COMPARISONS WITH CRIME
PREVENTION RESEARCH

Crime can be combatted by both threats of punishment and various social measures. In recent years, an enormous interest in the effects of crime prevention programs, especially in the field of juvenile delinquency, has developed in the United States. According to an estimate in a recent report to the Council of Europe, about one hundred million dollars will be spent on preventive research in the United States in the five year period beginning in 1965.[54] The major objective of the well known Cambridge-Somerville Youth Study was to test the hypothesis that delinquency can be prevented and good character development fostered by the presence of an adult "friend" who will stand by the boy through ups and downs and offer him the opportunities and moral guidance normally supplied by parents. The study disproved such an hypothesis.[55] Walter Miller's recent study of the impact of a "total-community" delinquency control project reached a similar conclusion.[56] The Miller study was concerned with three possible factors behind delinquent behavior: the community, the family, and the gang. The finding was that all the effort expended seemed to have a negligible impact.

There are marked similarities between rating the effects of crime prevention programs and assessing the results of changes in a penal system. In both cases a new set of conditions is introduced. The researcher is faced with the difficult task of assessing changes in criminality and, if such changes are found to exist, of judging whether the change is causally connected with the innovation. In a way, investigation of the effects of change in the penal system is usually a simpler task than estimating the effects of crime prevention programs. Such programs often are made up of a whole series of different activities so that even when we succeed in verifying that a change has resulted, we cannot know what parts of the program are instrumental in producing the effects. The same difficulties present themselves when changes in the repression of crime are introduced as part of a more extensive action plan. Let me give two examples, one from Denmark and the other from the United States.

During the first years of World War II, the number of bicycle thefts in Copenhagen increased substantially. By April 1942, the number of cases was three times the average annual number in the years before the war. The police decided to strike on several fronts so as to reduce criminality in this field. The police division which dealt with bicycle thefts was expanded. The courts were asked to be strict with bicycle thieves. In addition a meeting was arranged between the police and representatives of the leading Copenhagen newspapers, during which the head of the police detection division emphasized the serious consequences of the steadily increasing number of bicycle thefts. He argued that bicycle theft should be regarded as an asocial action of a markedly serious character and that it ought to be most strongly condemned by the public, especially in view of the shortage of bicycles during the war. The press was asked to advise citizens to secure their bicycles properly and to notify the police of any information which might be relevant to bicycle stealing. The public was also strongly warned against purchasing bicycles or parts of bicycles from unknown persons. The press found the subject matter to be "good news," and the plea to the public made the front pages. The newspapers then published daily notices about bicycle thefts, emphasizing the severity of the sentences. The campaign created a lively interest on the part of the public, judging from the vast number of reports to the police which in many cases led to a solution of the crime. The outcome of the campaign exceeded even the most optimistic expectations. The number of complaints during the subsequent months was less than half the number in April, and the decline proved lasting. The author of a report on this matter does not estimate which conditions were decisive in achieving the result.[57] It may have come about because of the increase of the police force, the intensification of the penalties, the change of attitude and the growing awareness of the public, or some combination of these.

The American example concerns a program carried out by the Waterfront Commission of the New York Harbor. When the Commission was established in 1953, conditions in the harbor were said to be deplorable:

> Large-scale stealing on an organized basis prevailed. Payrolls of steamship companies and stevedoring outfits were padded with "phantom" employees who collected paychecks for little or no work. Loan-sharking existed to a large degree. The investigative bodies also revealed corrupt payments by management to labor leaders to overlook legitimate labor rights. Guards were threatened with loss of life or job if too vigorous in their attempt to prevent stealing. Many union officials were proven to be criminals with extensive records. And there were many

other abuses. . . . It was felt that the Port of New York was in danger of losing its position of supremacy to which its natural advantages entitled it—all because of the mess of corruption, venality and general turbulence.[58]

The Waterfront Commission has operated both through strict law enforcement—assisted by a staff of well-qualified investigators—and by means of a series of control measures. The latter include registration or licensing of longshoremen, checkers, pier superintendents, hiring agencies, stevedoring companies, and steamship companies. Individuals who have extensive criminal records or who are tied directly to unsavory activity with the waterfront mob are denied registration or licensing. It is difficult to judge what part of the program has been most effective, but on the whole it appears to have been a remarkable success. This, at any rate, is the conclusion drawn by Thomas F. Coon:

> Not yet ten years of age, the Waterfront Commission of N. Y. Harbor has had a profound impact upon the Port of New York and the lives of the men who work the piers. It has assuredly improved the manner of living of the waterfront workers and has done much to foster a more efficient, economical, and safer movement of trade.[59]

However discouraging the conclusion may be, it seems clear that at present there is definitely more proof of the efficacy of repressive measures than of those crime preventing measures that have a different theoretical basis. An enthusiastic reformer some years ago argued: "If the community cannot afford both police and guidance experts, then it would do better to choose guidance experts." [60] On the basis of our present knowledge, this must be characterized as wishful thinking. Without a police force, guidance experts would have few opportunities to do their jobs.

ETHICAL PROBLEMS CONNECTED WITH
GENERAL PREVENTION

The use of any coercive measure raises ethical problems. This is so even when the motive rests upon the need to treat the person in question. To what extent are we justified in imposing upon someone a cure which he does not desire, and how are we to balance considerations in favor of his liberty against the need to eliminate the hazards he inflicts on society? Such problems are encountered in the public health services as well as in the exercise of criminal justice.

The conflict, however, assumes special proportions in connection with general prevention. It has often been said that punishment in this context is used not to prevent future violations on the part of the criminal, but in order to instill lawful behavior in others. The individual criminal is merely an instrument; he is sacrificed in a manner which is contrary to our ethical principles. This objection carries least weight in relation to general-preventive notions connected with legislation. The law provides, for example, that whoever is found guilty of murder is liable to life imprisonment or that whoever drives a car when he is intoxicated is to be given a prison sentence of thirty days. Such penal provisions have been laid down with an aim to preventing *anyone* from performing the prohibited acts. If we accept the provisions as ethically defensible, we also have to accept the punishment prescribed in each individual case. As H. L. A. Hart has stated:

> The primary operation of criminal punishment consists simply in announcing certain standards of behavior and attaching penalties for deviation, making it less eligible, and then leaving individuals to choose. This is a method of social control which maximizes individual freedom

within the coercive framework of law in a number of different ways.[61]

The question, however, comes to a head when the individual penalty is decided by general prevention considerations, in other words, exemplary penalties. I have previously mentioned the sentences given in connection with the race riots in London in 1958. According to the newspaper bulletins, the penalties assessed in the earlier cases were lenient, ranging from six weeks to three months. As the riots continued, the courts introduced heavy penalties of four years of imprisonment. "A groan of surprise came from the audience when the judgments were read," a correspondent reported. "On the galleries were seated the mothers of several of the boys, and they were led outside, weeping. Two of the boys were themselves totally paralyzed by the sentences and had to be helped out of the dock to their cells below the courtroom." The reporter continues: "After the encounters in West London, however, the race riots have waned away just as quickly as they started. The reason why they came to an end is undoubtedly the strong public reaction against racial persecution together with the resolute intervention of the police and the courts." [62]

If the correspondent is right,[63] the unusually heavy penalties in this case had a desirable effect, but the judgment is nevertheless felt to be ethically problematic. There is an element of ex post facto law involved in such sentences. Although the judge operates within the framework of the law, such sentences are not, in fact, applications of previously established norms. The judge establishes a norm to suit the situation. Nor does the result square with the ideal of equality before the law. The procedure calls to mind a practice which—at least according to historical novels—was commonly used in former times when a number of soldiers committed mutiny or similar grave violations: the commanding officer would have a suitable number of soldiers shot in order to instill fear and give warning, and the remaining soldiers were readmitted to service without penalty.

Such ethical doubts become even stronger if the individual sentence depends upon the kind of publicity—and hence the kind of preventive effect—which is expected. Suppose a judge is faced with two similar cases within a short interval. In the first case, the courtroom is filled with journalists, and the outcome of the trial is likely to become known to millions of readers. In the second case, the listener's benches are empty and, in all probability, the verdict will not spread far beyond the circles of those who are present in the courtroom. Is it defensible for the judge to pass heavy judgment in the first instance because the sentence is likely to gain much publicity and consequently bring about strong general-preventive effects, while the defendant in the second case is merely given a warning because punishment in his case would only mean personal suffering, and would not yield results from a social point of view? Such speculation upon the general-preventive effects of the individual sentence easily become tinged with cynicism and for ethical reasons this approach is only acceptable within very narrow limits.

Notes

1. See, *e.g.*, TAPPAN, CRIME, JUSTICE AND CORRECTION 247 (1960).
2. FEUERBACH, LEHRBUCH DES GEMEINEN IN DEUTSCHLAND GÜLTIGEN PEINLICHEN RECHTS 117 (5. Aufl. 1812).
3. A full account of the theories of general prevention is to be found in AGGE, STUDIER ÖVER DET STRAFFRÄTTSLIGA REAKTIONSSYSTEMET (*Studies in the System of Penal Sanctions*) (1939). See also AUBERT, OM STRAFFENS SOSIALE FUNKSJON (*The Social Function of Punishment*) (1954); KINBERG, BASIC PROBLEMS OF CRIMINOLOGY (1935); OLIVECRONA, LAW AS FACT (1939); and chapter 1, "General Prevention—Illusion or Reality?"

4. WOOTTON, CRIME AND THE CRIMINAL LAW 100–101 (1963).

5. *Ibid.*

6. 116 NORSK RETSTIDENDE 109 (1945).

7. It is particularly noteworthy that American criminological research, which is carried out mainly by sociologists, has not been concerned with general prevention.

8. BARNES & TEETERS, NEW HORIZONS IN CRIMINOLOGY 338 (2d ed. 1951).

9. ELLINGTON, PROTECTING OUR CHILDREN FROM CRIMINAL CAREERS 43 (1948), quoted in Ball, *The Deterrence Concept in Criminology and Law,* 46 J. CRIM. L., C. & P.S. 347, 351 (1955).

10. OMSTED, FORHANDLINGER VED DEN NORSKE KRIMINALIST-FORENINGS MÖTE 42 (1935).

11. TAPPAN, *op. cit. supra* note 1, at 246.

12. KOESTLER, REFLECTIONS ON HANGING 30 (1957) (with extracts of the speech of Chief Justice Ellenborough on May 30, 1810). See also 1 RADZINOWICZ, A HISTORY OF ENGLISH CRIMINAL LAW 231-59 (1948) (on "the doctrine of maximum security").

13. ZILBOORG, THE PSYCHOLOGY OF THE CRIMINAL ACT AND PUNISHMENT 78 (1954).

14. Ball, *supra* note 9, at 352.

15. Wilkins, *Criminology: An Operational Research Approach,* in SOCIETY—PROBLEMS AND METHODS OF STUDY 322 (Welford ed. 1962).

16. Six types of violations are discussed in chapter 1: police offenses, economic crimes, property violations, moral offenses, murder, and political crimes.

17. Military forces waging war in enemy territories might be regarded as constituting separate societies in which the pressure toward violations of law and the pressure toward conformity are both especially powerful. "There have been armies having no disciplinary punishments, no dungeons or execution platoons," says Tarde; "in every instance they soon became a horde." TARDE, PENAL PHILOSOPHY 480 (1912). The statement may contain some exaggeration, but there is a substantial measure of truth in it. In occupation armies characterized by strict discipline, as

for example the German army in Norway during World War II, plunder and rape are practically unknown, while such encroachments may assume great proportions when the discipline is weak. See RUSSELL, THE SCOURGE OF THE SWASTIKA 132–33 (1959).

18. GRASSBERGER, GEWERBS-UND BERUFSVERBRECHERTUM IN DEN VEREINIGTEN STAATEN VON AMERIKA 299 (1933).

19. KINBERG, *op. cit. supra* note 3, at 168–69.

20. See, *e.g.*, MODEL PENAL CODE § 4.01, comment at 158, appendix C at 184 (Tent. Draft No. 4, 1955).

21. The time element is important. Threats of punishment in the distant future are not as a rule as important in the process of motivation as are threats of immediate punishment.

22. See pp. 11–15.

23. See KINBERG, *op. cit. supra* note 3, ch. VI.

24. MANNHEIM, SOCIAL ASPECTS OF CRIME IN ENGLAND BETWEEN THE WARS 156–57 (1940).

25. TROLLE, SYV MAANEDER UDEN POLITI (1945).

26. TARDE, PENAL PHILOSOPHY 476 (1912).

27. TAFT, CRIMINOLOGY 322, 361 (rev. ed. 1950); Ball, *supra* note 9, at 350 n.11. See also Sellin, *L'Effet Intimidant de la Peine*, [1958] REVUE DE SCIENCE CRIMINELLE ET DE DROIT PÉNAL COMPARÉ 579, 590 (1960), concerning an experiment of the New York police in 1954.

28. 1958 SOCIALA MEDDELANDEN 329–30.

29. See Toby, *Is Punishment Necessary?*, 55 J. CRIM. L., C. & P.S. 332, 333–34 (1964).

30. INNSTILLING FRA STRAFFELOVRAADET OM ADGANGEN TIL AA AVBRYTE SVANGERSKAP 26 (1956).

31. See, *e.g.*, WILLIAMS, THE SANCTITY OF LIFE AND THE CRIMINAL LAW 209–12 (1957).

32. *Id.* at 213–20.

33. See *id.* at 236; 2 EXCERPTA CRIMINOLOGICA 73 (1962). See also, MEHLAN, INTERNATIONALE ABORTSITUATION (1961).

34. 2 STEPHEN, THE HISTORY OF THE CRIMINAL LAW OF ENGLAND 81 (1883).

35. Walker & Argyle, *Does the Law Affect Moral Judgments*, 4 BRITISH J. CRIM. 570 (1964).

36. STEPHEN, A GENERAL VIEW OF THE CRIMINAL LAW OF ENGLAND 99 (1863).

37. TROTSKY, TERRORISME ET COMMUNISME 68 (1920).

38. NORWEGIAN MOTOR VEHICLE CODE OF 1926, § 17.

39. See ANDENAES & HAUGE, UAKTSOMT DRAP I DE NORDISKE LAND 78–79 (1966); Schram, *Trafikkulykker og Alkohol,* 1954 MOTORTIDENDE 10–15. Of 7,967 traffic accidents in 1951, the driver was under the influence of alcohol (more than 0.05% alcohol in the blood) in 114 cases. Of 194 fatal accidents, the driver was under the influence of alcohol in 10. In 1960, the figures were 310 and 11 respectively. It should be noted that since blood tests are taken only in cases where there is a suspicion of alcohol consumption, the figures given are minimum figures.

40. BEUTEL, EXPERIMENTAL JURISPRUDENCE 366 (1957).

41. *Ibid.*

42. It has been contended that only a system of penalties representing *just retribution* will exert the desired influence on public morals. See the authorities referred to in ANDENAES, THE GENERAL PART OF THE CRIMINAL LAW OF NORWAY 64 n.12 (1965). Just retribution, according to this school of thought, is not the goal of punishment; it is the means which, socio-psychologically speaking, is most effective in securing obedience. Such general hypotheses are difficult to validate or negate.

43. For a first rate and up-to-date survey, see HOOD, RESEARCH ON THE EFFECTIVENESS OF PUNISHMENTS AND TREATMENTS (Report to the European Council No. DPC/CDIR 9, 1964).

44. BEUTEL, *op. cit. supra* note 40, at 366.

45. A strong increase in policing activities may, at least temporarily, lead to an increase in the number of convictions and perhaps in the number of reports to the police as well.

46. TARDE, PENAL PHILOSOPHY § 87 (1912).

47. KINBERG, *op. cit. supra* note 3, at 127–38.

48. 3 RADZINOWICZ, HISTORY OF ENGLISH CRIMINAL LAW (1957).

49. MOORE & CALLAHAN, LAW AND LEARNING THEORY: A STUDY IN LEGAL CONTROL (1943).

50. BERRIEN, PRACTICAL PSYCHOLOGY 454–55 (1946).

51. Related to the author by Professor Inkeri Anttila, Helsinki. See also the 1954 experiment of the New York police, note 27 *supra*.

52. AUBERT, *op. cit. supra* note 3, at 177.

53. See 3 EXCERPTA CRIMINOLOGICA 23 (1962) [Abstract of Aronson & Carlsmith, *The Effect of Severity of Threat on the Devaluation of Forbidden Behavior*, 17 THE AMERICAN PSYCHOLOGIST 300 (1962)].

54. CHRISTIE, RESEARCH INTO METHODS OF CRIME PREVENTION (Report to the European Council No. DPC/CDIR 10, 1964).

55. POWERS & WITMER, AN EXPERIMENT IN THE PREVENTION OF DELINQUENCY: THE CAMBRIDGE-SOMERVILLE YOUTH STUDY (1951).

56. Miller, *The Impact of a "Total-Community" Delinquency Control Project*, 10 SOCIAL PROBLEMS 168 (1962).

57. 3 GLUD, KAMPEN MOD FORBRYDELSEN 369 (1951).

58. Coon, *Waterfront Commission Investigator*, 3 EXCERPTA CRIMINOLOGICA 369–70 (1963).

59. *Id.* at 371.

60. Ball, *The Deterrence Concept in Criminology and Law*, 46 J. CRIM. L., C. & P.S. 347 (1955), citing LANDIS, SOCIAL POLICIES IN THE MAKING 185 (1952).

61. HART, PROLEGOMENON TO THE PRINCIPLES OF PUNISHMENT 21–22 (1960).

62. *Aftenposten*, Sept. 20, 1958, p. 20.

63. See WOOTTON, CRIME AND THE CRIMINAL LAW 100–101 (1963).

III

DETERRENCE AND SPECIFIC OFFENSES

Deterrence should not be treated as a monolithic problem. General propositions accepting or rejecting deterrence ought to belong to the past. The question is not whether punishment has deterrent effects, but rather under what conditions and to what extent the deterrent purpose is effected.

It is important initially to distinguish between the deterrent effect of the threat of punishment (general deterrence) and the deterrent effect of the imposition of punishment (special deterrence).[1] Professor Chambliss has suggested that the distinction between general and special deterrence, perhaps useful in the abstract, is difficult to maintain in empirical research and may, in fact, obscure more than it clarifies.[2] His own discussion, however, demonstrates that failure to make the distinction may lead to mistaken conclusions. Chambliss concludes, on the basis of research showing high rates of recidivism among drug addicts, that drug addiction, like murder, is relatively unaffected by either the threat or imposition of punishment.[3] This statement may be correct if restricted to those users who have already become addicts, since the great physiological need for drugs may vitiate the deterrent effect of punishment. But it is not correct to presuppose, as does Chambliss, that the limited success in the treatment of drug addicts necessarily suggests a similar failure to deter non-addicts and drug dealers. In fact, statistics concerning recidivism among drug addicts reveal nothing about the deterrent effect of drug laws on non-addicts and drug dealers. Howard Becker's study of the marijuana user may be instructive.[4] Becker identifies three stages in the career of a marijuana user: beginner, occasional user, and regular user. The beginner is faced with two major obstacles created at least in part by the drug laws. First, he must overcome his fears of criminal penalties and social disapproval. Second, even if he overcomes these fears, he must locate a supplier. Since sale of the drug is subject to severe criminal penalties, its distribution is confined to illicit, not readily available sources.[5] Thus, even though special deterrence with regard to the convicted drug addict may fail, general deterrence may operate effectively to prevent potential users from becoming addicts.

In discussing deterrence it is also necessary to distinguish among offenses. Common sense tells us that the threat of punishment does not play the same role in offenses as different as murder, rape, tax evasion, shoplifting, and illegal parking. The different offenses vary greatly as to both motivation and extralegal restraints upon commission of the crime. Chambliss agrees that deterrent effects differ according to the type of offense, but makes a general distinction between expressive and instrumental acts. An act such as drug use or murder is expressive in that it "is committed because it is pleasurable in and of itself and not because it is a route to some other goal." [6] Acts such as parking violations and shoplifting are, on the other hand, instrumental. According to Chambliss, the available research suggests that expressive acts are resistant to punishment as a deterrent, whereas instrumental acts are more likely to be influenced by the threat or imposition of punishment.

The analytical value of Chambliss' distinction is

doubtful. It does not seem self-evident that expressive acts are less influenced by social sanctions than are instrumental acts. Experience from social intercourse shows that the fear of even mild social sanctions often leads to the suppression of expressive acts (for example, yawning, picking one's nose, or crying out angrily).

Moreover, the distinction does not seem very clear. For instance, Chambliss considers the use of narcotics a typically expressive act. It may seem pedantic to object that taking the drug is instrumental in bringing about the ultimate effects of the drug. But certainly the purchase or possession of the drug is instrumental in relation to the later use. Criminal acts to obtain the drug or to obtain money to buy it are even more clearly instrumental. Yet experience seems to show that the desperate addict is deterred no more from committing these instrumental acts than he is from committing the expressive act—use of the drug. Thus, what leads to a lack of deterrent effect is not the expressive character of drug use, but rather the overwhelming motivating power of the addiction. That carefully planned acts are more easily deterred than those that result from a sudden, emotional impulse is an old proposition. The latter acts are probably more commonly labeled expressive. Apart from this distinction, however, referring to the act as expressive or instrumental does not seem to give a significant clue to the problem. A much more detailed analysis is needed.

I have previously discussed the general deterrent effect of punishment in relation to six broadly defined categories of offenses: violations of police regulations; violations of economic legislation; crimes against property; moral offenses; murder; and political crimes.[7] In this article I shall consider three more specific offenses: infanticide, criminal abortion, and drunken driving. The discussion is limited to general deterrence, using the term "deterrence" broadly to include the possible moral or habit forming effects of criminal laws.

INFANTICIDE

Infanticide, typically an unmarried woman's murder of her newborn child, was one of the great problems of the criminal law in the eighteenth century. Erik Anners, a Swedish legal historian, has provided useful information on the crime in his study of criminal law reforms during the Age of Enlightenment.[8] Although rare until the end of the sixteenth century, infanticide became more common during the seventeenth and eighteenth centuries and came to be regarded as a major social evil. The increased frequency of infanticide seems to have been attributable primarily to the development of stronger religious and legal proscriptions of extra-marital relationships. These pressures created a strong temptation to hide the pregnancy and kill the child after its birth.

When the infanticide rate increased, due partly to the law itself, the threat of severe punishment was considered to be the only remedy. Therefore, partly for deterrent reasons and partly because of the religious view that a life must be paid for with a life, infanticide became a capital crime. Between 1759 and 1778, 217 of the 617 executions in Sweden were for infanticide. Those executed were usually from the poorer classes, and more often than not were countryside housemaids. The situation in other European countries was basically the same.

In the late eighteenth century, King Gustav III of Sweden [9] attempted to reduce the punishment of infanticide. He argued, perhaps to disarm his opponents, that capital punishment was an inadequate deterrent. He urged that a woman convicted of infanticide be first flogged and then imprisoned, perhaps for life. On the anniversary of the crime she was to be flogged before the common people. The King thought that this would create disgust for the crime and fear of the punishment. Opposition from conservative jurists and theologians, however, prevented enactment of these reforms. Not until 1861 was capital punishment for infanticide abolished, although granting of pardons had ended executions for the offense a generation earlier.[10]

It is difficult to ascertain the frequency of infanticide in eighteenth century Sweden. In 1773, the Swedish Supreme Court stated that infanticide and abortion are "yearly committed in such numbers over the whole country that the country loses considerably in population due both to the crime itself and to the ensuing penalty." Crime statistics and execution records, however, do not support so strong a statement. The Supreme Court must therefore have presumed that infanticide was committed much more frequently than the statistics indicated, and some evidence suggests that this assumption was correct.[11] It is also possible that the punishment itself, severe even to people of that era, contributed to the feeling that infanticide was a great problem.

Veli Verkko, a Finnish statistician, has investigated the frequency of infanticide in Finland and Sweden during the eighteenth century, when the two countries were united and ruled by the same law.[12] His investigations, based on an evaluation of death statistics, reveal that the frequency of illegitimate births was greater in Sweden, but that the frequency of infanticide was greater in Finland. In Finland, the infanticide rate was highest in those counties in which the frequency of illegitimate births was lowest. His fairly plausible explanation is that strong sexual mores and social bias against the unwed mother resulted in fewer pregnancies among unmarried women, but also caused many of those who did have an illegitimate child to commit infanticide. He concludes that: "[w]e have here an example of the peculiar phenomenon under which a rigid morality can have a criminogenic, i.e., crime-producing effect." [13]

Infanticide was still prominent in the crime statistics of

the nineteenth century.[14] In the 1860's, there were annually between ten and twenty convictions for infanticide in Norway; and in Sweden, with approximately double Norway's population, there were between thirty and forty. In the twentieth century, infanticide has gradually become less frequent and the penalty has consistently become less severe. In Norway, between 1957 and 1966, seven persons were found guilty of infanticide. In five of these cases prosecution was waived, and in the two that were brought to court the defendants received a suspended sentence of imprisonment for the minimum term of one year.[15] In Sweden, during the same period, eight defendants were convicted, but the sentences are not specified in the statistics.

What explains this decline in the frequency of infanticide? It is unlikely that increased knowledge of contraceptives is a major cause of the decline. The number of children born out of wedlock has not, in a long term perspective, dramatically decreased. In Norway, in 1866, 4,310 children, or about eight percent of the total live births, were illegitimate. A hundred years later the number was 3,285, about five percent of all live births. Thus, increased knowledge of contraceptives appears largely to have been neutralized by relaxation of sexual mores during this century. Furthermore, there is reason to believe that knowledge of contraceptives has been slow in reaching the levels of society in which infanticide was most prevalent.

Two further hypotheses seem more plausible as explanations for the decline in the infanticide rate. First, the more liberal attitude of society towards extra-marital relationships coupled with better care of illegitimate children serve to mitigate the stigma which formerly attached to an unwed mother. Second, the solution to an unwanted pregnancy, previously provided by infanticide, is now abortion. Both of these factors probably have had an effect, although a detailed discussion of them is outside the scope of this article.

In view of the decline in the infanticide rate during the last century, can one conclude that the severe eighteenth century penalties for infanticide were useless brutality without deterrent effect? Anners seems to come to this conclusion,[16] but he may be too bold. One cannot reject out of hand the possibility that more unhappy women might have resorted to infanticide had the penalty been less severe. But neither can such a hypothesis be proven. What one can safely conclude, however, is that a social problem, previously thought to require drastic criminal penalties, has been solved in other ways. It is also likely that most people today would find it easier to accept an increased infanticide rate than to impose the severe penalties once thought to be required by religion and deterrence. History reveals that strong beliefs in deterrence, particularly when combined with the moral or religious belief that sin should be punished, can produce results which later generations will consider unnecessarily brutal.

ABORTION

The abortion situation in most western countries is characterized by strict laws, weak enforcement, and a high rate of criminal abortions. The number of illegal abortions is astronomic compared to the number of prosecutions or convictions for the crime. It is often said that the criminal law in this area is ineffective in that it does not have an appreciable effect on the abortion rate. This notion is reflected in a recent paper by B. J. George:

> Will even the most wildly liberal abortion statute make much difference in the incidence of abortion? I doubt it. The gross rate of abortions probably remains unaffected by efforts at legal regulation of the practice: the chief

question is how many of the abortions actually performed will be done openly in hospitals or clinics.[17]

Sanford Kadish states that:

[As a] hard fact [the] abortion laws do not work to stop abortion, except for those too poor and ignorant to avail themselves of black-market alternatives, and . . . the consequences of their retention is probably to sacrifice more lives of mothers than the total number of foetuses saved by the abortion laws.[18]

These statements illustrate how even excellent scholars can be guilty of sloppy thinking, probably due in this case to the widespread skepticism among criminologists with regard to the efficacy of the criminal law.

It is undoubtedly true that many women who desire to terminate a pregnancy but who cannot do so legally successfully procure an illegal abortion. But it seems obvious that this is not true of all women who would have an abortion if available on request. Some women may be too helpless, too passive, or too poor to find and use the alternatives open to the more active and resourceful. In other cases, a woman who would have an abortion if available on request may hesitate to make the rounds from one doctor to another begging for help or to permit a "quack" to perform the abortion.

These conclusions seem obvious and are supported by statistical evidence. Follow-up studies of women whose requests for abortion were denied show that although a great number of them subsequently obtain a criminal abortion, this is by no means true for all. A Danish study revealed that eighty-one percent of the 3,700 women whose requests for abortion were denied or withdrawn in 1958 and 1959 completed their pregnancies.[19] The percentage among housewives was considerably higher than among office workers: eighty-eight percent and seventy percent respectively. Swedish inquiries showed similar results.[20] A Norwegian study made before the abortion law was liberalized showed that only thirty-six percent of the women whose applications for abortion were denied completed pregnancy.[21] Married women were more likely to bear the child than unmarried women: thirty-nine percent and twenty-eight percent respectively. A study under the present law showed that sixty-eight percent of the women whose applications were denied completed pregnancy: eighty-one percent of the married applicants and fifty-four percent of the single applicants.[22] It thus seems clear that the percentage of women who complete unwanted pregnancies depends on such factors as marital and occupational status and on the more or less easy availablity of criminal abortions. The stronger the motivation for abortion and the easier the access to criminal abortion, the higher the percentage of women who will solve their problem in this way.

Another possible method of assessing the effect of abortion legislation is to compare the change in legal abortions following a liberalization of the law with the trend in the birth rate. In places, such as the Scandinavian countries, where more liberal laws changed the accepted grounds for abortion only moderately, the number of legal abortions is too small to have a noticeable effect on the birth rate.[23] In contrast, the number of legal abortions has increased dramatically in those Eastern European countries where post-war legislation legalized abortion at the mother's request.[24] Concurrent with the increase in legal abortions was a sharp decline in the birth rate. In Hungary, the number of legal abortions in 1964 exceeded the number of live births by almost forty percent.[25] On the other hand, in East Germany and Albania, the two Eastern European countries that had not legalized abortion, there was a modest increase in the birth rate.

While the relationship between the birth rate and liberalized abortion law is not simple, an open-minded study of the statistics seems to support Professor Tietze, who,

after a thorough study of the available information, concluded that the legalization of abortion has had a depres-
sant effect on the birth rate in most Eastern European
countries.[26] The most striking example is Romania where
abortion on demand was legalized in 1957 but again prohibited in 1966. The birth rate had declined from 24.2
per thousand in 1956 to 14.3 per thousand in 1966. It is
estimated that the number of abortions in 1966 was four
times the number of live births. The reasons for the repeal
of the 1957 law were stated in the preamble to the 1966
law: "[there has been] great prejudice to the birth rate and
the rate of natural increase." [27] The effects of the new law
were dramatic. The birth rate jumped from 14.3 per thousand in 1966 to 27.3 per thousand in 1967, 26.7 per thousand in 1968, and 23 per thousand in 1969.[28] It should be
noted that in conjunction with the reversed abortion policy, the government increased family allowances and ceased
official importation of contraceptives. In Bulgaria, a tight-
ening of abortion legislation in December, 1967, led to an
increase (albeit not as great as in Romania) in the birth
rates in 1968 and 1969. One can confidently conclude that
the increased number of legal abortions in some of the
East European countries includes some cases where previously a criminal abortion would have been performed
and others in which the woman would have completed her
pregnancy.[29]

Paradoxical as it may seem in view of the high rate of
illegal abortions, there are probably few areas where so
little enforcement has so much effect as in the field of
abortion. This is due primarily not to the effect of the
criminal law on the motivation of women who want to
terminate pregnancy, but rather to the effect on the medical profession. Since safe abortion requires a doctor, prefer-
ably in a hospital, and since the medical profession on
the whole is quite susceptible to the threat of law and the
censure of society, the legal prohibition may prevent the

mother from obtaining abortion without respect to her own attitude. Moreover, abortion is an area of the law in which the law may itself have a moral impact. If abortion were legalized, women would find it easier to overcome the feeling of guilt that now often accompanies the act. It is probably of no great significance whether the mother is herself subject to punishment. It is enough that abortion is criminal. Legalization of abortion may also result in carelessness in the use of contraceptives, producing more unwanted pregnancies and increased demand for abortions. The effect of abortion laws is obviously dependent on a variety of factors including religious beliefs, attitudes of the medical profession, knowledge and availability of contraceptive techniques, and social and economic conditions.

Abortion and infanticide are both the result of pregnancy which is viewed as a threat to the future life or happiness of the mother. But infanticide is, in contrast to abortion, a simple, primitive crime which does not require expert assistance. Moreover, the moral inhibitions against infanticide are much greater than those against abortion. For these reasons the effect of criminalization on the two types of conduct differs markedly.

To avoid misunderstanding, it should be pointed out that the deterrent effect of making abortion criminal is not a decisive argument against the liberalization of abortions. It can be argued that the mother ought to have the right to decide for herself whether to complete a pregnancy. Assuming that an unwanted child is a greater evil than a terminated pregnancy, it seems logical to conclude from the usual rise in the abortion rate after liberalization that there is a legitimate need for abortion which is not met under present law. But the indications of a deterrent effect are not without impact on the argument over liberalization: the policy problem would be different and easier to solve if there were no deterrent effect, that is, if it could be shown that the effect of liberalization would be only to legalize abortions which would be performed anyway.

DRUNKEN DRIVING

For many years the Scandinavian states have had strict legislation against drunken driving, coupled with strict enforcement policies. In Norway, for example, the law prohibits driving when the blood alcohol level exceeds .05 percent. Any person suspected of drunken driving must submit to a blood test. Upon conviction, the driver's license is revoked for at least one year and, in addition, the consistent policy of the courts has been to impose a prison sentence. This strict policy seems to have had a considerable effect on driver attitudes with regard to driving under the influence of alcohol, and drunken driving now causes a very small percentage of highway accidents.[30] However, this legislation has been in force since a time when there were far fewer automobiles and accidents than today. It is therefore impossible to demonstrate statistically the impact of the legislation.

The situation is different in Great Britain, which recently adopted a new highway safety act.[31] The new legislation retained existing provisions which led to conviction only in cases involving a high degree of intoxication but added a new offense: driving with an undue proportion of alcohol in the blood. The prescribed limit is eighty milligrams of alcohol in one hundred milliliters of blood (.08 percent). If the police have reasonable cause to believe that a driver has been drinking or has committed a moving traffic offense, they may ask the driver to take a breath test. The police may always request a breath test if the driver has been involved in an accident.[32] If the test indicates that the driver's blood alcohol content is probably above the legal limit, he may be arrested and taken to the police station. There the driver is requested either to submit to a blood test or, if he refuses, to furnish two urine specimens for analysis. Failure to cooperate with these requests renders the driver liable to the same penalties that attach to driving with the proscribed blood alcohol content. Upon conviction for the new offense, the driver's license is automatically revoked for one year, except in extraordinary circumstances, and the driver is also subject to a fine of up to £100, four months imprisonment, or both.

An intensive publicity campaign, beginning two weeks prior to the effective date of the Act (October 9, 1967) and continuing for four months, accompanied passage of the new law. The campaign, estimated to have cost nearly £350,000, was particularly intense in the beginning and during the December holiday season. News coverage and comments in the press, radio and television provided additional publicity for the new law. As a result, there was great public awareness of the new law, and unusual interest in highway safety in general.

Highway accident statistics were carefully compiled to gauge the effect of the new legislation. This is one of the few instances in which an effort has been made to learn the precise effects of a new policy. According to official figures, highway accidents decreased substantially after the Act took effect.[33] The following table is compiled from those figures.

PERCENTAGE DECREASE IN HIGHWAY CASUALTIES IN GREAT BRITAIN,
OCTOBER TO DECEMBER, 1967, COMPARED WITH
SAME PERIOD IN 1966

	Oct.*	Nov.	Dec.	Oct.–Dec.	Christmas
Fatalities	17	20	33	23	36
Seriously injured	15	15	22	17	30
Slightly injured	11	13	20	15	

* Figures for October represent the period after the Act took effect.

In the first nine months of 1967 there was no consistent trend in the incidence of the highway accidents; there was an increase over the previous year during some months and a decrease in others. Overall, there was a two percent decrease in casualties as compared with 1966. Total traffic was estimated to have increased from 1966 by five percent in October, two percent in November, and to have decreased one percent in December. Neither the figures for 1966 nor those for the first nine months of 1967 reflect any remarkable change in comparison with previous years. In the 1950's and 1960's there had been a slow but steady upward trend in highway casualties. The annual number of fatalities had increased from about 5,000 in the early 1950's to approximately 8,000 during the period from 1964 to 1966.

After the passage of the Highway Safety Act of 1967, there was a larger decrease in serious accidents than in minor accidents. This result is in harmony with the findings of previous highway accident research showing that accidents involving drivers with blood alcohol levels over .08 percent tend to be more serious than the average accident.[34] Different drinking and driving habits during the holidays may explain the great reduction during the Christmas season. While changes in weather conditions may influence the figures for each month, the consistency of the figures is remarkable.

A striking pattern emerges if the accidents are correlated to the periods of the day in which they occurred. During working hours (8 A.M. to 6 P.M.) the decrease is slight: two percent of fatal and serious accidents in October and November; seven percent in December. Between 8 P.M. and 4 A.M. the figures were thirty-six percent in October, thirty-eight percent in November and forty-one percent in December. For the early morning hours considered alone they were even higher. The inevitable conclusion is that, in this socially important area, new legislation has had a considerable impact on people's behavior, at least temporarily.[35]

A study of about half of the fatal accidents in Great Britain in December, 1964, and January, 1965, showed that thirty percent of the fatally injured drivers had more than .05 percent blood alcohol content. Twenty-three percent of the fatally injured drivers had more than .08 percent blood alcohol content and twelve percent had more than .15 percent. Seventy-five percent of the drivers killed between 10 P.M. and 2 A.M. had at least .05 percent blood alcohol content compared with ten percent of the drivers killed between 6 A.M. and noon.[36] These figures do not mean, of course, that drinking was the cause of the accident in all cases, but the implications are obvious.

Several alternative hypotheses which might be thought to explain the decrease in highway accidents in Great Britain deserve discussion. It may be argued that increased awareness of the dangers of drunken driving rather than the threat of punishment led to the reduction in the number of accidents. This theory credits the publicity campaign rather than the law itself for causing the decrease. This argument, however, does not appear to be supported by the facts. There had been long-standing public discussion of the problem of drunken driving, and the publicity campaign began two weeks before the new law took effect. Yet, in the first eight days of October, 1967, there was a reduction in highway casualties (compared with the same period in 1966) of only two percent—the same reduction obtained in the first nine months of 1967. In that portion of October after the Act took effect, the reduction was twelve percent. The decrease in fatalities was one percent in the eight days of October before the Act took effect and seventeen percent for the remainder of the month. Moreover, surveys conducted among drivers in September, 1967, and January, 1968, showed that drivers' toleration of drinking and driving and their opinion of the amount they could drink without affecting their driving remained substantially unchanged.[37] It seems clear that the dramatic reduction in highway accidents is directly attributable to the new legislation. The report of the surveys concluded that the publicity campaign had been valuable only in the sense that it made drivers aware of the new law.

Even if this conclusion is accepted, it does not necessarily follow that the explanation for the decrease in highway accidents is the effect of the new law on alcohol consumption before driving. An alternative hypothesis is that drivers, expecting increased police surveillance during the period immediately following the effective date of the new Act, exercised greater caution in driving quite apart from the Act's effect on alcohol consumption. It may well be that some part of the reduction of accidents is due to this factor. However, the distribution of the decrease in accidents according to time of day indicates that the most important factor was change in drinking and driving habits.

An important question is whether the effects of the new law are permanent. Other cases exist where an initial reduction in the commission of the proscribed offense, resulting from a new law accompanied by intensive publicity, has been followed by an eventual return to the previous level.[38] There is some indication of a similar development in Great Britain. In the last three months of the first year in which the Act was in effect, fatalities were nine percent less than in the previous year, seriously injured seven percent and slightly injured seven percent.[39] While these decreases are less impressive than those for the months immediately following the effective date of the Act, the development is somewhat ambiguous. As stated above, December is probably the month in which the most social drinking occurs. In December, 1967, the decrease from the 1966 level was thirty-three percent and in December, 1968, the decrease was thirty-two percent. The figures for seriously injured were twenty-two and nineteen percent and for slightly injured, twenty and eighteen percent. Thus, the reduction in the level of casualties for this month was practically the same as in the first year of the law's operation. It is possible that the other safety measures introduced by the Ministry of Transport during the year influenced these figures. Nevertheless, the Ministry's conclusion "that a fair proportion of the reductions are being maintained, although it is clearly too early to assess the long term effects," [40] seems well founded. Post mortem examinations of fatally injured drivers revealed that the percentage of such drivers with blood alcohol content of over .08 percent fell from a previous average of twenty-eight percent to fifteen percent in the first year after the effective date of the Act. [41]

For the first twelve months after the effective date of the Act, the total reduction in casualties compared to the previous year was ten percent. This represents 1,152 fewer fatalities, 11,177 fewer seriously injured and 28,130 fewer slightly injured. Opinion polls indicate that a majority of the population favors the new Act. But when fifteen percent of drivers who are fatally injured in highway accidents have blood alcohol content of over .08 percent and eleven percent have over .15 percent, a serious drunken driving problem still exists. It would be interesting to have comparable information from the Scandinavian countries, where drunken driving legislation is older and stricter.

A decrease in the deterrent effectiveness of the new law with the passage of time can be interpreted in three ways:

1. The publicity in connection with the Act created an exaggerated fear of detection for drunken driving. Later, drivers began to make a more realistic assessment of the risk of detection, and consequently the deterrent effect was weakened. The law had been "oversold." In addition,

many loopholes in the law gradually became public knowledge, thus reducing the deterrent effect.

2. The motivating force of a risk is dependent not only on the intellectual knowledge of the risk, but also on the degree of awareness. If, for example, one witnesses a traffic accident, his awareness of the risks of driving is greatly increased. In the same way, it can be assumed that the risk created by a new law is fresh in the minds of drivers, especially if enactment is accompanied by intense publicity. This high degree of risk awareness is gradually weakened, even when no reassessment of the risk is made. It is impossible to maintain the same level of publicity after the initial period of the Act's operation, and even if this were attempted, public sensitivity would probably be reduced when the publicity lost its news interest. Thus, a certain decrease in the "shock effect" of new legislation must be expected as a normal development.

3. To the extent that the immediate reduction of highway casualties is due not to a changed pattern of alcohol consumption, but to the general driver expectation of more intense traffic control, the effect of the new law will necessarily be temporary.

These considerations could have been evaluated more effectively had surveys of drivers been made periodically. This would have been an important supplement to the accident statistics and would have revealed more about the psychological effects which led to the decreases. The survey research that has been done failed to cover such questions as how drivers assess the risk of detection.

The foregoing discussion has been concerned primarily with the awareness of the risk of punishment. However, I do not intend to imply that the effects of the new legislation are a result only of fear. Although survey research does not indicate a change in attitudes toward drinking and driving per se,[42] the desire to obey the law may well have played a considerable role in the change in behavior. Therefore, it cannot be assumed that similar legislation, even when enforced in the same manner as in Great Britain, will have the same effects in a country whose citizens view obedience to the law differently. My personal view, however, is that the major factor in the success of the British legislation is mere deterrence. Creation of similar awareness of risk in a different society would have similar results if the drinking patterns and the social characteristics of the drivers were approximately the same.

Statistical evidence of the general preventive effects of punishment is scarce. What broader conclusions can be drawn from the British experience? Why do the British statistics yield the unequivocal results which are usually so difficult to obtain? Two points should be mentioned.

First, driving under the influence of alcohol differs from traditional crimes in that conduct not previously criminal has been made criminal, and it is therefore possible to measure the total impact of the new law. Crimes such as murder, robbery, rape, and burglary remain substantially the same from one generation to the next. Changes relevant to the deterrent effect of the law usually concern the level of penalties or the level of enforcement. With such crimes, instead of measuring the total impact of the criminal provisions, there is the more difficult task of measuring the marginal effect of a change in the penalty or the degree of enforcement.

Second, in this case statistics of highway accidents provide an independent measure of the effects of the law. It is thus possible to avoid many of the difficulties of measuring the extent of violations. When the scope of a penal law is extended or contracted, it is theoretically possible to measure the total impact of the extension or contraction of the law. But "before" and "after" tests in these situations are especially difficult because criminal statistics do not provide a "before" measure for conduct that is now criminal or an "after" measure for conduct that has ceased to be a crime.

It should be noted that the number of highway accidents resulting from drinking may not be presumed to vary directly with the number of violations of the drunken driving laws. The effect of the law often may be that the driver reduces his consumption in order to decrease the risk of detection, even though his blood alcohol content remains higher than the maximum legal limit. Because the risk of an accident increases as the amount of alcohol increases, such reductions in consumption may be very important in relation to the goals of the law. If the legal limit is low, a high proportion of fringe violators may be of minor importance for highway safety. Since the aim of the law is to promote highway safety, the influence of the law on the number of accidents is a better measure of its efficacy than would be "before" and "after" statistics on the number of drivers whose blood alcohol content exceeds the limit.

Since the change in accident statistics shows the total impact of the new legislation, it is a poor basis for forecasting the effects of changes in the level of penalties or in the stringency of enforcement. Norwegians generally accept the proposition that nonsuspension of prison sentences imposed for drunken driving has been very important in promoting the deterrent effect of the law. In Great Britain, the sentence usually consists of a fine and temporary loss of the driver's license. This contrast gives reason for questioning the importance of prison sentences. Perhaps fines and license revocation can achieve almost the same results as prison sentences; but further discussion on this point would require a much more thorough study.

For several reasons, a stronger deterrent effect may be expected from drunken driving laws than from laws against many other types of offenses. Driving under the influence of alcohol is not restricted to a criminal subculture, and it is not subject to severe moral condemnation. Nor is it behavior triggered by strong emotions. The decision whether or not to drink is usually made deliberately, as a rational choice; and the motivation to commit the offense is not strong. The law interferes only slightly with personal liberty. It asks the citizen neither to stop drinking nor to stop driving. It merely prohibits combining the two activities. Thus, the drunken driving situation is one in which common sense tells us that the risk of punishment can be expected to have more effect than in the case of many other offenses. This point should not, however, be overstated. There is no standard of the normal or average crime to which drunken driving is an exception. Every offense must be considered separately. Indeed, the motivational situation in many socially important types of offenses may be more similar to drunken driving than, for example, to murder or rape.

As enforcement of a law becomes more effective and penalties for its violation become stricter, the class of lawbreakers becomes more abnormal. It is no doubt correct that drunken driving was common throughout the population before the passage of strict criminal sanctions. Distribution of the violators is not so widespread after the passage of the new legislation. The composition of the class of drunken drivers will be altered. Instead of a fairly random sample of drivers, the drunken drivers will be primarily the problem drinkers and those with previous records for drunken driving—people less amenable to being deterred. This fact must be taken into account in forecasting the effect of any increase in the level of enforcement or punishment of an offense which is already strictly enforced and punished. He who invests in increased severity, has to expect diminishing returns.

Notes

1. On the question of terminology see *Appendix 1* and Hawkins, *Punishment and Deterrence: The Educative, Moralizing, and Habituative Effects,* 1969 Wis. L. Rev. 550.

2. Chambliss, *Types of Behavior and the Effectiveness of Legal Sanctions,* 1967 Wis. L. Rev. 703, 704 n.3.

3. *Id.* at 708.

4. H. Becker, Outsiders ch. 4 (1963).

5. Hauge gives a similar description from Oslo. The use of marijuana and hashish is relatively widespread in some circles in Oslo, but even if one could identify these circles, it would be a long time before they would trust him enough to sell the drugs to him. If the individual were conspicuously different from those in the drug-using circles, they would probably never sell drugs to him. Hauge, *Narkotikamisbruk som Gruppefenomen* (The Use of Narcotics as a Group Phenomenon), Prismet 161, 163–64 (1969).

6. Chambliss, *supra* note 2, at 708, 712.

7. See chapter 1.

8. Anners, Humanitet och Rationalism (Humanitarianism and Rationalism) (1965).

9. King of Sweden, 1771–1792.

10. K. Olivecrona, Om Dödsstraffet (On Capital Punishment) 53–54 (1891).

11. See Anners, *supra* note 8, at 142, 207–08.

12. Verkko, *Barnamorden och Sexualmoralen i Sverige-Finland på 1700-Talet,* Nordisk Tidsskrift for Strafferet 35 (1946).

13. *Id.* at 45.

14. The development can be illustrated partly by the crime statistics and partly by the death statistics. Between these two sources there are, at least in Norway, discrepancies which are difficult to explain. Unfortunately, because of several rearrangements of the statistics, I have not been

able to present them in a coherent graph of the development.

15. Information on the sanctions is provided by the Prison Department of the Ministry of Justice.

16. ANNERS, *supra* note 8, at 154.

17. George, The Law Governing Abortion, April 28, 1968, p. 12 (unpublished paper delivered at The University of Chicago Conference on Abortion).

18. Kadish, *The Crisis of Overcriminalization,* 374 ANNALS 157, 163 (1967).

19. BERETNING OM MÖDREHJAELPSINSTITUTIONERNES VIRKSOM-HED 45 (1963).

20. Ekblad, *Induced Abortion on Psychiatric Grounds,* ACTA PSYCHIATRICA ET NEUROLOGICA SCANDINAVICA, supp. 99, ch. VIII (1955).

21. INNSTILLING FRA STRAFFELOVRAADET OM ADGANGEN TIL AA AVBRYTE SVANGERSKAP (Report from the Penal Code Commission on Abortion) (1956).

22. Strőm, *Svangerskapsavbrot i visse hőve,* TIDSSKRIFT FOR DEN NORSKE LAEGEFORENING 761, 769 (1969).

23. In the Scandinavian countries the total number of legal abortions is 5–10% of the number of live births.

24. The Soviet Union does not publish statistics on abortions and is not included in the discussion of Eastern European countries.

25. Tietze, *Abortion in Europe,* 57 AM. J. PUB. HEALTH 1923, 1930 (1967).

26. Tietze, *The Demographic Significance of Legal Abortion in Eastern Europe,* 1 DEMOGRAPHY 124 (1964). Professor Tietze also comments that in Hungary in 1952 and 1953, before the liberalized abortion legislation, concerted efforts were made to enforce the existing abortion laws. "These efforts led to an increase in births in 1953 and 1954." *Id.*

27. Tietze, *supra* note 25, at 1931.

28. H. David, Family Planning and Abortion in the Socialist Countries of Central and Eastern Europe, 1970, at 21, 127 (mimeo.). In Table 14 the changes in the birth rate after the 1966 law was passed can be followed from month to month. *Id.* at 131.

29. In Japan the great increase in the number of legal abortions performed after passage of liberal post-War legislation has been accompanied by a marked decline in birth rates. Tietze, *Some Facts About Legal Abortion,* in HUMAN FERTILITY AND POPULATION PROBLEMS 223, 228–29 (R. Greep ed. 1963).

30. See pp. 60–61 with note 39.

31. Road Safety Act 1967, c. 30 (effective Oct. 9, 1967).

32. The proposal in MINISTRY OF TRANSPORT, ROAD SAFETY LEGISLATION, 1965–66, CMND. No. 2859, at 11 (1965), to give the police the power to make random tests did not receive the approval of Parliament. "The system of random checks, however unpalatable, is evidently the only way in which the new law can be enforced for it is usually only at levels in excess of 150 mg./100 ml. that a motorist's conduct exhibits obvious signs of unfitness." 1966 CRIM. L. REV. (Eng.) 65, 67. In the light of later experience, this seems to be too pessimistic a view.

33. Ministry of Transport Press Notices, No. 892 (Dec. 19, 1967), No. 78 (Feb. 8, 1968), and No. 157 (Mar. 21, 1968).

34. See, *e.g.,* BORKENSTEIN, CROWTHER, SHAMATE, ZIEL & ZYL-MAN, THE ROLE OF THE DRINKING DRIVER IN TRAFFIC ACCIDENTS 176–77 (1964) [hereinafter cited as BORKENSTEIN].

35. A paper issued by the ministries involved before the law came into effect said that it had been calculated that in the absence of driving after drinking, the number of drivers involved in accidents would be reduced 6%. (Drinking and Driving—Background Information [issued on behalf of Ministry of Transport, Home Office, Scottish Development Department, Welsh Office].) That figure, which was considerably exceeded since the Act took effect, was apparently based on a computation by the Road Research Laboratory from the findings of the Michigan "Grand Rapids Survey," BORKENSTEIN, *supra* note 34. The survey was based on comparisons between drivers involved in accidents and a random sample of drivers. The report from the Ministry of Transport, *supra,* summarizes research findings of the Road Research Laboratory concerning the frequency of drinking among people involved in highway accidents. The Laboratory's report gives

12.6% as the reduction in total accidents which would have occurred if drivers with blood alcohol content of .08% or more had been prevented from driving. *Id.* at 167–69. The method of computation of the Road Research Laboratory is explained in Alsop, *Drinking Drivers,* 170 NEW SOC'Y 12 (1965), and in Alsop, *Alcohol and Road Accidents,* Road Research Laboratory Report No. 6 (1966).

36. Older & Sims, *Blood Alcohol Levels in Road Accident Fatalities Occurring in Great Britain During December 1964 and January 1965,* Road Research Laboratory Report No. 32 (1966). In the United States, blood tests performed on fatally injured drivers have revealed extremely high proportions of drunken drivers. A study of single vehicle accidents in Westchester County, New York, showed that 49% of the drivers had blood alcohol content of .15% or more, and that an additional 20% had blood alcohol content between .05% and 1.5%. Haddon & Bradess, *Alcohol in the Single Vehicle Fatal Accident, Experience of Westchester County, New York,* in ACCIDENT RESEARCH 208, 211 (1964). See also McCarroll & Haddon, *A Controlled Study of Fatal Automobile Accidents in New York City,* in ACCIDENT RESEARCH 172 (1964).

37. Sheppard, *The 1967 Drink and Driving Campaign: A Survey Among Drivers,* Road Research Laboratory Report LR 230 (1968).

38. See, *e.g.,* Middendorff, *Desirable Developments in the Administration of Justice,* II COLLECTED STUDIES IN CRIMINOLOGY RESEARCH, COUNCIL OF EUROPE 45, 59 (1968). Judge Middendorff discusses the German Second Road Traffic Act which became effective January 2, 1965.

39. The figures are taken from a communication to the Norwegian Committee on Traffic Research from the Road Research Laboratory, Ministry of Transport, and are for the months of July, August, and September, 1968.

40. Ministry of Transport, The Road Safety Act 1967 and its Effect on Road Accidents in the United Kingdom (undated mimeo.).

41. Road Research Laboratory Report No. 32, *supra* note 36, at 3-4 & Table IV (referring to a Road Research Laboratory Report by R. F. Newbay in course of preparation).
42. Road Research Laboratory Report LR 230, *supra* note 37. This sort of change may come at a later stage, when the initial success of the law in reducing the accident rate has become known among drivers.

IV

THE MORAL OR EDUCATIVE INFLUENCE
OF CRIMINAL LAW

DIFFERENT VIEWS OF PUNISHMENT

Punishment is a traditional means of influencing people's behavior, from the rebuke or slap on the fingers of the small child to the heavy sentences of the courts in cases of serious crime. In criminal law theory a distinction is made between the effects of a threat of punishment (general deterrence) and the effects of actual punishment on the punished individual (special deterrence). In this article I shall be concerned only with general deterrence: the effect of the threat of punishment.

Two extreme positions often emerge from the literature on the subject. One is the position of Jeremy Bentham, who considered man to be a rational being choosing between possible modes of action on the basis of a calculation of risks of pain and pleasure. The consequence of this model is clear enough: If we make the risk of punishment sufficient to outweigh the prospect of gain, the potential lawbreaker will, as a rational man, choose to stay within the limits of the law.

The other extreme, often represented by psychiatrists, discards this model as unrealistic. When people remain law-abiding, they maintain, it is not because of fear of the criminal law, but because of moral inhibitions or internalized norms. If an internal restraint is lacking, the threat of punishment does not make much difference since criminals do not make rational choices, calculating gain against the risk of punishment; they act out of emotional instability, lack of self-control, or because they have acquired the values of a criminal subculture. For the sake of convenience, I shall speak of this as the psychiatric model, although not all psychiatrists would agree with it. The extreme representatives of this way of thinking tend to look upon the idea of general deterrence as a kind of superstition used by lawyers to defend their outmoded system of criminal law or as a cloak to conceal and rationalize their retributive feelings. In my view, both extremes are equally mistaken, or to put it in a more friendly way, each represents only part of the truth.

The danger of generalization
Different kinds of offenses vary so greatly in motivation that it is obvious that the role of the criminal law in upholding norms of conduct is very different for every offense. Any realistic discussion of general deterrence must be based on distinctions between various types of norms and on an analysis of the particular circumstances motivating transgression.[1] In general terms it can only be stated that general deterrence works well sometimes and works poorly or not at all at other times.

People react differently
The threat of punishment is directed to all of us, but it affects us differently. With regard to a certain kind of criminal conduct, the population could be divided into three groups: (*a*) the law-abiding man, who does not need the threat of the law to keep him on the right path; (*b*) the potential criminal, who would have broken the law if it had not been for the threat of punishment; and (*c*) the criminal, who may well fear the law but not enough to

keep him from breaking it. It is in the intermediate group, the potential criminal, that the deterrent effect of punishment is at work.

We do not know the proportions of persons in these categories, but they will obviously vary by offense and even by geographical area. Nor do we have any easy means of identifying the citizens who belong to the different groups. Moreover, the groups are not static but change with changing conditions. Under exceptional conditions, e.g., war or other serious crises, the number of actual as well as potential offenders may increase many times.

The moral or educative effect of the criminal law

Both the Bentham model and the psychiatric model are concerned with the direct deterrent effects of the law. However, punishment is not only the artificial creation of a risk of unpleasant consequences but also a means of expressing social disapproval. And this official branding of conduct may influence attitudes quite apart from fear of sanctions. The term "general deterrence" is in fact too narrow, insofar as it excludes this moral or educative influence. I prefer the continental tradition of speaking of the *general-preventive effects* of punishment. From the legislator's perspective, creating moral inhibitions is of greater value than mere deterrence because the former may work even in cases where a person need not fear detection and punishment. Moreover, a successful inculcation of moral standards may result in social pressure towards acceptable behavior even on persons who have not been influenced personally by the moral message of the law.

It should be noted that when I speak of moral or educative influence, in accordance with traditional terminology, no value judgment is implied. The expression is used only to designate an influence on attitudes and behavior which emanates from the law but is not based on fear. I do not assume that this influence is always a good or desirable one. Bad laws can influence attitudes just as can good laws. Hawkins has criticized the use of the term "moral" in this wide sense.[2] He prefers to speak about the socializing effects. This seems to me to be a terminological question of no great significance. The most neutral terminology would perhaps be to speak about the attitude-shaping influence of criminal law.

It may seem somewhat artificial to single out for study the influences on human behavior emanating from the system of criminal justice, since these influences at most represent just one thread in a complicated web. The necessity for research into the subject stems from the practical tasks of the legal profession. We are constantly confronted with the problem: What can be achieved by means of criminal law—and at what cost? Traditional legal methods do not provide an answer beyond crude guesswork based on common sense.

DIRECT MORAL INFLUENCES

It would not be quite fair to state that the spokesmen of classical deterrence theory totally overlooked the moral influence of criminal law. Thus Beccaria in his discussion of the punishment for different categories of crimes makes the following statement:

> If the same punishment be decreed for killing a pheasant as for killing a man, or for forgery, all difference between those crimes will shortly vanish. It is thus that moral sentiments are destroyed in the heart of man. . . .[3]

This, in fact, expresses a strong belief in the potentialities of criminal law to influence moral attitudes in society. And even Bentham mentions the power of punishment to act as a "moral lesson." [4] English authors such as Stephen [5] and Kenny [6] express similar viewpoints. Furthermore, the idea of moral or educative effects of criminal law are implied when "reinforcement of social values" is mentioned among the goals of criminal law. But above all the doctrine has been developed by German and Swedish authors. Sometimes this moral influence is considered more important than the direct deterrent influence. The German criminologist Hellmuth Mayer thus asserts that "the basic general preventive effect of criminal law does not at all stem from its deterrent but from its morality-shaping force. . . . Nothing is so convincing to man as power, provided it appears as expression of a moral order." [7] In Swedish literature, Lundstedt was an extreme and eloquent representative of the same view. The purely deterrent effects of criminal law were, according to him, "of quite minor significance, hardly worth mentioning" as compared with the moral influence.[8] In the same vein, the Canadian J. D. Morton professes that "the most important function of the criminal law is that of education or conditioning." [9] It is often asserted that this effect takes place only when punishment has the character of just retribution. Just punishment "attaches to the criminal act a taboo-conception and has the effect that in most cases the possibility of committing the prohibited act is not at all considered." [10]

These statements are made with great confidence, but there does not seem to be much research or practical experience to substantiate them. On closer analysis it seems that there may be various aspects to the moral or educative influence of criminal law. The following is an attempt to explicate these different aspects.

Respect for the formal law
It is a common although far from universal attitude in society that legal commands or prohibitions ought to be obeyed even by those who may be critical of the law in question. This feeling of obligation depends upon a respect for legitimate authority. If the conduct in itself is considered reprehensible, the stamp of the law reinforces

this feeling. If the act is morally neutral, respect for the law operates alone.

Plato tells that Socrates out of respect for the law drank the cup of poison instead of following the offer of his friends to bribe his custodians so that he could escape. But Socrates was no ordinary man. In most people respect for formal law is probably relatively weak, in some it is totally lacking, while others may even hold the law in contempt. Dollard et al. contend: "Within any given state internal hostility to the symbols of authority is a common feature of social life. It is manifested alike by labor leaders and capitalists as well as by groups which hope for revolutionary change." [11] A modern American textbook for police recruits maintains that "there exist in almost every community, a certain number of citizens who resent authority in any form, delight in community disturbances and do all they can to obstruct the conduct of police business." [12] The distribution of such attitudes could be explored by survey research.

Attitudes to law compliance may vary from one society to another and they may change over time. European observers of American society have often remarked that respect for legislation is less in the United States than in most European countries. "The legislative mill grinds as it does in European countries, but the average American cares little what comes out of it." [13] Similar statements are found in works of American scholars. Taft expressed it this way: "American culture does not demand or approve obedience to all laws. . . . The slogan 'obey the laws' is never meant to be taken without qualification. It is but a slight exaggeration to say that *most* conservative people believe that *other* people should obey *most* of the *most important* laws *most* of the time." [14] This may be related both to the highly pluralistic character of American society and to the way the political machinery works. Legislation is looked upon, perhaps quite realistically, not as a solemn and authoritative statement of the "will of the state" but as the outcome of a very mundane power structure. For the young, underprivileged black in the ghetto, "law" seems not to be the object of much positive feeling. The Riot Commission in its 1968 report cited a deep hostility between police and ghetto communities as a primary cause of the disorders of 1967. "The policeman in the ghetto is a symbol not only of law, but of the entire system of law and criminal justice. As such, he becomes the tangible target for grievances against shortcomings throughout that system." [15]

A certain degree of respect for the formal law is probably essential for the smooth functioning of society. Where it is lacking, law enforcement agencies play a role similar to that of an occupying army in foreign territory, a comparison which has been made often enough with regard to the law enforcement agencies in the ghettos of American cities. Experience shows that an occupying army may be able to create a high degree of order and compliance if it is prepared to use sufficiently harsh terror methods. But such a reign of terror is fundamentally different from the system we are used to in democratic societies.

An absolute respect for formal law may also represent a danger. Blind deference to authority is not considered a virtue in democratic countries. Such blind obedience was the psychological background for many German war crimes and has often been mentioned as a criticism against the German people during the Nazi period. In his experiments on obedience, Milgram called his findings disturbing, since submission to authority led normal people to perform harsh acts.[16]

Criminal law as a moral eye opener
It is possible that the fact that a certain act has been labelled criminal can make the citizens more aware of its socially harmful character. Thus the Swedish author Thyrén says that in some cases the effect of the threat of punishment is

"not so much that it deters the individuals through fear, but that it opens their eyes to the socially dangerous character of the act and makes their conscience more sensitive on this point." [17] Cameron has described this eye opening effect among shoplifters.[18] When a shoplifter is apprehended, he realizes more clearly that he has committed a criminal and shameful act. Before the arrest, the shoplifter had not thought of himself in these terms.

Possibly a similar although certainly much weaker effect may result from knowledge that an act is declared criminal. Such effects could perhaps be expected as a consequence of penal legislation against driving under the influence of alcohol or concerned with negligent homicide. The law may bring drivers to reflect on the dangerous and irresponsible character of driving under the influence of alcohol. For the time being at least, opinions on this matter have to remain rather speculative. A recent British survey of drivers before and after a new law on drunken driving offers some relevant data.[19] The law, which went into effect in October 1967, was accompanied by an extensive publicity campaign and led to a substantial decrease in the accident rate. It may be asked whether this was due solely to the deterrent effect of the new law or whether a change in moral attitudes toward drunken driving had taken place. Drivers were questioned about their opinions on the effect of drinking on driving ability and about their attitudes toward drinking and driving (e.g. should people who drink and drive be disqualified from driving?). The answers to both types of questions showed little change from the first to the second survey. It seems likely that it was the deterrent effect of the new law which was important in bringing about a change in behavior, not the publicity campaign and moral eye-opener effects of the new law. The publicity campaign seems to have been of value only in the sense that it made drivers aware of the new law.

*Punishment as authoritative statements
about wrongdoing*

Our attitudes toward different modes of behavior are, to a high degree, the result of suggestive influences from society. Legislation and the machinery of justice send out messages to the public. Punishment expresses social disapproval, and it does this in a discriminatory way: The heavier the punishment, the stronger the disapproval. If the individual is disposed to accept the evaluations of the authorities, he will be influenced by way of suggestion. Nigel Walker speaks of the "declaratory function" of the criminal law,[20] Joel Feinberg of the "expressive function" of punishment.[21]

In view of our general knowledge of how attitudes are formed and sustained, it does not seem probable that the direct influence of the legal norms is very strong as compared with influences of the various primary groups to which the individual belongs. Walker even states that "legislation must be one of the weakest influences that could be imagined." But, since primary groups transmit legal norms, there may be a cumulative effect. If the law succeeds in influencing some individuals, the effects may spread to others as a result of social interaction.

Schwartz and Orleans conducted a field experiment to test how a sanction threat and a moral appeal influence normative orientation and actual behavior with regard to the payment of federal income taxes.[22] One group of taxpayers was asked questions designed to remind them of the penalties they might risk by tax evasion. Another group was asked questions designed to accentuate moral reasons for compliance. Two control groups had either a neutral interview or none at all. The findings, based on analysis both of questions about normative orientation and of actual taxpaying behavior, are somewhat difficult to interpret. They suggest that the punishment threat has some effect on normative orientation, at least in some social groups, but that the conscience appeal in most groups was more forceful. The same applied to the effects on actual taxpaying.

Walker and Argyle also tested the hypothesis that criminal law has moral effects.[23] Answers to a survey questionnaire about the morality of attempted suicide showed that knowing that the penal provision against attempted suicide had been repealed did not result in a less strict view than not knowing about the change; indeed, there was a slight but statistically insignificant tendency in the opposite direction. Other questions regarding the moral significance of acts such as litter-dropping, public drunkenness, prostitution, and use of obscene language yielded parallel findings.

However, these research studies were only concerned with short-term effects. Most believers in the moral effects of punishment have relied on long-term effects. Further, Walker and Argyle excluded from their sample that small, but by no means negligible, minority who believe that the law automatically governs the morality of the conduct. Finally, Walker and Argyle's research deals only with the morality or immorality of acts on the borderline of criminal law, not with the degree of moral reprobation incurred by acts commonly rejected as immoral and deserving of punishment. It might be argued that punishment has greater power to support and reinforce commonly held moral judgments than it has to create a previously nonexistent moral condemnation. While the evidential value of the findings is limited, they do arouse some skepticism concerning the claims of the strong believers in the moral potentialities of criminal law.

Historical experience points in the same direction. If criminal law continues to express moral attitudes which represent the views of former generations about such matters as sexual behavior, the normal development will be that the penal provisions will become less and less enforced and eventually will be repealed. Many such provisions can continue to exist only so long as no real attempt is made to enforce them. At least in these areas of behavior moral attitudes decide the content of criminal law, and not the other way round. Experience also shows that moral indignation can flow freely without the reinforcement of criminal law. In England, incest was not an offense until a statute was enacted in 1908. Even so, it is not likely that moral indignation towards incest was less intense in the England of Queen Victoria than it is today.

A practical and important question remains as to whether actual sentencing policy for a certain type of offense can influence the public's evaluation of that kind of conduct. Imprisonment is normally imposed only for somewhat more serious offenses and it expresses a high degree of social disapproval. Is it possible through the application of prison sentences to make certain offenses more reprehensible in the eyes of the public? Experience does not supply us with a simple answer. On the one hand, Clinard in studying black-market violations during World War II found that imprisonment was a more effective penalty than fines.[24] His survey of businessmen showed that they feared imprisonment much more than fines. This fear was motivated not only by the inconvenience of being incarcerated but also by the moral stigma attached to a prison sentence. Clinard also reports that in the districts where the Office of Price Administration regulations were strictly enforced, compliance was more prevalent than where enforcement was lax.

On the other hand, it seems that the public shows discrimination in its attitudes toward prison sentences. If the motivation of the offender is considered unselfish or honorable, sentencing does not influence the public's judgment of the offense or the offender, even though the public may accept the sentence as justified. The Scandinavian countries have had extensive experience with passing short prison sentences on those apprehended driving under the influence of alcohol. In Norway, more people go to prison for this one misdemeanor than for all felonies put together. The sentence carries with it some stigma, but the stigmatizing effects are not strong enough to make any appreciable change in the offender's employment possibilities or his social relationships. A recent study by Klette of a group of fifty drivers with no previous criminal records, sentenced to from one to two months' imprisonment for drunk driving, showed that the offenders in no case had to change employment because of the prison sentence, although the employers in all cases but one knew of the offender's stay in prison.[25] It should be added that the convicted drivers did not consider themselves "criminals" and they kept to themselves in prison. In some cases the wife of the offender reacted strongly, but otherwise the effects of the prison sentence on social and personal relations seemed to be insignificant.

The effects described above are closely related. In practice it may be difficult to distinguish among them; they all seem to revolve around the concept of *legitimate authority*. However, in the section "Respect for the Formal Law," I have noted that the individual does not change his view on the morality of the act per se as a result of the legal provision; if he now considers the act wrong or immoral, it is only because he generally considers it wrong to act in violation of the law. In "Criminal Law as a Moral Eye-Opener" and "Punishment as Authoritative Statements About Wrongdoing," I have described situations where the law *has* changed the moral attitude of the individual toward the act. The difference between the two is that the effect described in the former occurs as a result of the individual's personal thinking and evaluation, whereas the effect described in the latter is due merely to suggestive influence.

A tentative conclusion on the basis of available evidence would be that only within narrow limits is it possible for criminal law to directly influence moral attitudes in society, at least in a short-term perspective.

This statement refers to the situation in a democratic, pluralistic society which enjoys wide freedom of discussion. The situation may be different in an authoritarian setting where the state apparatus has power over the schools, social organizations, press and other mass media, and where all these instruments for indoctrination can support the legal system. In his treatise *Justice in the USSR* Berman speaks about the educative role of Soviet law and Soviet Courts.[26] This idea of educating the citizens by way of law and courts has found expression in the Russian Code on Court Organization which states in article 3:

> By all its activity a court shall educate citizens in the spirit of loyalty to the Motherland and to the cause of Communism, and in the spirit of undeviating execution of Soviet laws, of a protective attitude toward socialist property, of observance of labor discipline, of an honorable attitude toward state and social duty, and of respect for the rights, honor, and dignity of citizens and for rules of socialist communal life.[27]

INDIRECT MORAL INFLUENCES

So far we have described the direct moral influences of punishment. The indirect moral influences are probably considerably stronger.

Punishment as reducing and neutralizing bad example

Experience shows clearly that bad example, when it goes unpunished, can be infectious. With such matters as illegal parking and other trivial offenses it is easy to observe how the lack of enforcement may lead to mass infringement and the total breakdown of compliance to regulations. But the bad example mechanism has a much wider field of application. Thus, time and again cases are reported of large-scale theft by the employees of a company. The more violations, the fewer qualms the individual feels. The unthinkable is not unthinkable any longer when one sees one's comrades doing it. Why should one be honest when others are not? The risk seems less real, and, at the same time, moral inhibitions are broken down. In the same way, a branch of the public administration can be penetrated by corruption. The danger of bad example is probably greatest in situations such as these where the individual learns of offenses committed by others whose circumstances are similar to his. But it is not restricted to such situations. The increasing frequency of hijacking international airliners in recent years gives an interesting illustration of the contagious nature a certain kind of criminal conduct may have when not effectively met by penal sanctions.

The machinery of criminal law works in two ways to counteract this effect. First, it reduces—through deterrence and in other ways—the number of bad examples. Second, it makes the bad example less attractive. Awareness of criminal law in action works as a vaccination against the temptation to follow the example. There may be different theories about the psychological mechanisms, but about the fact itself there can hardly be any doubt.

To get an idea of the importance of example one can try to visualize the situation if criminal law or its enforcement were paralyzed, not for a few hours or days as in the case of police strikes, but permanently. To begin with, the criminal elements would commit more crimes and more openly than before. Their example would be followed by individuals on the moral borderline who up to now had been kept in check by fear of the law. And by a kind of chain reaction more people would gradually be involved in criminal activities, especially of the acquisitive kind. It may be that moral inhibitions are sufficiently strong today to keep most people from committing serious crimes, but whether this would hold true in a society without a machinery of criminal justice seems a more doubtful proposition.[28] Perhaps there is a great deal of truth in the statement of Ekelöf:

> If the moral standard of the people is to be maintained, it is in my opinion not sufficient that people get their standards of conduct inculcated in their childhood; they need to see them applied by those around them throughout life and to conceive of them as an integrated part of the prevailing social mores. From the cradle to the grave man must be exposed to constant moral propaganda. And in this propaganda the activity of the machinery of justice plays an important role.[29]

Criminal law shapes the framework for moral education

While punishment can prevent the breakdown of established moral norms by serving as a continuing re-education or reinforcement function throughout the life cycle, the criminal law system may also have indirect effects on a person's moral education during the crucial years of his early education and development. This education takes place primarily in the family, in school, and in other small groups, but it is not independent of conditions in society outside these groups. The existence and working of criminal law and its machinery provide a general framework which must necessarily have deep-rooted consequences for the moral climate of society and the moral education to which children are exposed. It would be difficult to teach honesty, nonviolence, and similar positive values in a society where these rules were openly and commonly broken without punishment. Moreover, the existence of criminal law and the machinery of justice may motivate parents and others in similar authority roles to impress more strongly upon the child those moral rules. The parents will teach the child not to steal not only because they consider theft immoral but also because the consequences for the offender may be serious. Many parents probably use references to police and prison as means of communicating to children the absolute necessity of "going straight."

The Norwegian educator Nordland pointed out the parallel between the functions of discipline in an educational setting and of criminal law in the greater society.[30] In analogy to the concept of general prevention, she speaks about a general or group-oriented discipline which is maintained through fixing a set of rules and applying sanctions against violation. The children learn thereby the limits of acceptable behavior, and they learn to respond to symbols of what represents forbidden conduct. For the sake of group discipline it may be necessary to apply the prescribed sanction even in cases where it is not considered necessary to prevent repetition by the violator himself. On the other hand, there are children who do not react adequately to the normal system of discipline and who, therefore, have to be given individual treatment. In practice there may be a tension between those two principles, as there is in criminal law between considerations of general prevention and considerations of individual treatment.

Summary and conclusion
Let me try to sum up the tentative conclusions of this chapter:

1. What is generally called the moral or educative effects of criminal law consists of several components, which may have varying force in different fields.

2. The respect for formal law, independent of sanctions, does not have a strong motivating force for most people, and is easily pushed aside when coming into conflict with self interest.

3. The potentialities of criminal law to create or in-

tensify a moral censure of certain types of conduct, either by an eye-opener effect or by exerting a suggestive influence, are very limited. It seems that moral sentiment shapes criminal law more than the other way round.

4. Criminal law has an important function in upholding the moral inhibitions of the individual by counteracting the demoralizing effect of bad examples.

5. Furthermore, criminal law has an important function in shaping the framework for the moral education of the young.

Criminologists, on the whole, have not taken a great interest in the general effects which criminal law and the system of criminal justice have for human behavior. They have been much more interested in the individual offender, his personality and environment, and the effects of the criminal sanction on him. Often the idea of general-preventive effects of criminal law has been looked upon as outmoded dogma, which ought to be discarded in favor of a more realistic and scientific view of man.

My own perspective is very different. I consider law, and not the least criminal law, as one of the fundamental socializing influences. I tend to think that a modern, highly industrialized and urbanized society of Western type could hardly function without criminal law, police, and a reasonably effective system of criminal justice. This system does not work simply through fear, but exerts its influence on human thought and behavior in varied and more subtle ways. Because these influences permeate society in so many ways, they are difficult to isolate and measure. In this respect the institution of punishment is in the same situation as other fundamental institutions of society.

Notes

1. See chapters 1 and 3.
2. Hawkins, *Punishment and Deterrence: The Educative,*

Moralizing and Habituative Effects. 1969 WIS. L. REV. 550.

3. BECCARIA, AN ESSAY ON CRIMES AND PUNISHMENTS 139 (1770).

4. BENTHAM, AN INTRODUCTION TO THE PRINCIPLES OF MORALS AND LEGISLATION 184 (1879).

5. STEPHEN, A HISTORY OF THE CRIMINAL LAW OF ENGLAND, Vol. 2, 79 (1883).

6. KENNY, OUTLINES OF CRIMINAL LAW, 15th. ed. 35 (1936).

7. MAYER, DAS STRAFRECHT DES DEUTSCHEN VOLKES 26, 32 (1936).

8. LUNDSTEDT, PRINCIPINLEDNING 30 (1920); TILL FRÅGAN OM RÄTTEN OCH SAMHÄLLET 105 (1921).

9. MORTON, THE FUNCTION OF CRIMINAL LAW 43 (1962).

10. MAYER, STRAFRECHT, ALLGEMEINER TEIL 23 (1953).

11. DOLLARD ET AL., FRUSTRATION AND AGGRESSION 85 (1939).

12. GERMANN ET AL., AN INTRODUCTION TO LAW ENFORCEMENT (1962) [Quoted after J. D. Lohmann in 1967 FED. PROBATION 31 (4), 22].

13. KINBERG, BASIC PROBLEM OF CRIMINOLOGY 168–69 (1935).

14. TAFT, CRIMINOLOGY 234 (1942).

15. REPORT OF THE NATIONAL ADVISORY COMMISSION ON CIVIL DISORDERS (Paperback ed.) 299 (1968).

16. Milgram, *Behavioral Study of Obedience,* 67 J. AB. SOC. PSYCH. 371–78 (1963); *Some Conditions of Obedience and Disobedience to Authority,* 18 HUMAN REL. 57–76 (1965).

17. THYRÉN, STRAFFRÄTTENS ALLMÄNNA GRUNDER 72 (1907).

18. CAMERON, THE BOOSTER AND THE SNITCH 161–64 (1964).

19. Sheppard, *The 1967 Drink and Driving Campaign: A Survey among Drivers,* ROAD RESEARCH LABORATORY REPORT LR 230 (1968).

20. Walker, *Morality and the Criminal Law.* 11 (3) HOWARD J. 209 (1964).

21. Feinberg, *The Expressive Function of Punishment,* 49 THE MONIST 397 (1965).

22. Schwartz & Orleans, *On Legal Sanctions.* 34 U. CHI. L. REV. 274 (1967).

23. Walker & Argyle, *Does the Law Affect Moral Judgments?* 4 BRITISH J. CRIM. 570 (1964).

24. CLINARD, THE BLACK MARKET (1952).

25. Klette, *Några resultat från tre rattfylleriundersökningar jämförda med trafiknykterhetskommittens lagförslag,* NORDISK TIDSSKRIFT FOR KRIMINALVIDENSKAB 119–35 (1964).

26. BERMAN, JUSTICE IN THE USSR (1963).

27. BERMAN, SOVIET LAW AND CRIMINAL PROCEDURE 429 (1966).

28. In addition to the experiences of police strikes and similar situations cited in chapter 2, pp. 50–51, a more recent example is the police strike in Montreal in 1969. A Canadian newspaper (*Toronto Star,* October 8, 1969) had these comments:

> "Though it lasted only a day, Montreal's wildcat police strike has taught some bitter lessons to all of Canada.
>
> "*The first* concerns the issue of strikes in public services. . . . Within a few hours a great city had been reduced to anarchy, with rioters and vandals running amok with no one to stop them.
>
> "*The second* lesson was the fragility of that pattern of order and decent behavior that we call civilization. It was to be expected that, with no policemen in sight, professional criminals would go about their work with enthusiasm. But what was really frightening was the way in which normally law-abiding people indulged in looting, brawling and setting fires. . . .
>
> "It was, of course, only a minority of citizens who let themselves be carried away. But there are enough of them in Montreal or in any great city to bring life back to the jungle unless there is at all times a reliable system of law and order. . . ."

It may well be that this commentary is overdramatized, but that similar effects would take place in the case of a permanent paralysis of criminal justice seems highly probable.

29. EKELÖF, STRAFFET, SKADESTÅNDET OCH VITET 54 (1942).

30. E. Nordland, *Allmennprevensjon og disiplin i oppdragelsen,* NORDISK TIDSSKRIFT FOR KRIMINALVIDENSKAB, 220–37 (1966).

V

THE MORALITY OF DETERRENCE

THE PROBLEM

Deterrence, both general and special, is one of the traditionally accepted aims of the criminal law. This chapter will consider only general deterrence: the deterrent effect of the threat of punishment. This concept will be used in its broad sense, including the so-called moral or educative effects of criminal law,[1] thus corresponding to the continental term "general prevention."

Legislators as well as criminal courts often base their decisions on considerations of general deterrence. But punishment on this ground has been attacked time and again in the literature as unjust. Bittner and Platt, for example, contend that "punishment on the basis of deterrence is inherently unjust. For if an example is made of a person to induce others to avoid criminal actions then he suffers not for what he has done but on account of other people's tendency to do likewise."[2] This criticism, frequently raised, seems to rest on Kant's moral principle that man should always be treated as an end in himself, not only as a means for some other end.[3]

Ethical questions cannot be conclusively resolved by analysis and argument. In the last resort we have to take a stand based on personal sentiment, or, in more lofty terms, on personal values. There is no possibility of empirical verification of these values. All we can do is discuss the implications and consistency of our principles.

The Kantian principle has a persuasive ring, but can hardly be treated as a binding rule without closer scrutiny. As with other abstract principles it lends itself to different interpretations, and it is difficult to evaluate the validity of the principle without examining its practical applications. Realistically, societies often treat people in ways designed to promote the good of society at the expense of the individual concerned. Military conscription may be the prime example of this phenomenon which also finds expression in quarantine regulations, confinement of dangerous mentally ill patients, and detention of enemy citizens in wartime. Thus, the Kantian principle, in practical application, is of doubtful value. Moreover, even if we accept the principle, it hardly leads to a general conclusion that punishment based on deterrence is contrary to the demands of justice.

The theory of general deterrence has, however, often been stated in terms which make it a rewarding target of attack on ethical grounds.[4] Reverend Sydney Smith's statement of the theory in the 1830's provides a good example:

> When a man has been proved to have committed a crime, it is expedient that society should make use of that man for the diminution of crime; he belongs to them for that purpose. Our primary duty, in such a case, is to treat the culprit that many other persons may be rendered better, or prevented from being worse, by dread of the same treatment; and, making this the principal object, to combine with it as much as possible the improvement of the individual.[5]

This statement considers only the application of punishment in the individual case and does not relate punishment to the general rule of law. For a closer analysis of this relationship it may be useful to distinguish between general-preventive considerations as a basis for *legislation* and as a basis for *sentencing*.[6]

CONSIDERATIONS OF GENERAL PREVENTION IN LAWMAKING

The legislature's prescriptions, for example, of life imprisonment for murder, thirty days imprisonment for tax evasion or drunken driving, or a heavy fine for speeding, are general provisions directed toward everyone. They attempt to motivate every potential violator to conform. Infliction of punishment for one of these violations is a consequence of the legal provision; it does not require special justification in each case. Punishment is essential to the law's effectiveness; without its application the law would be an empty letter. Thus, if it is ethically justifiable to issue penal laws in order to regulate human conduct, it cannot be ethically unjust to apply the law in the individual case. It cannot be said that the offender "suffers not for what he has done but on account of other people's tendency to do likewise." [7] He suffers for what he has done in the measure prescribed by the legislature. As H. L. A. Hart has put it, the primary operation of criminal punishment consists of announcing certain standards of behavior and attaching penalties for deviation, and then leaving individuals to choose. This, he asserts, is a method of social control which maximizes individual freedom within the framework of the law.[8]

The connection between the criminal provision and its application was stated forcefully by Feuerbach.[9] The aim of the penal law, he says, is deterrence. The aim of the application of punishment is to fulfill the command of the law so that it does not contradict itself. Feuerbach discussed and accepted Kant's principle; he argued that this principle does not conflict with the application of punishment as a consequence of the law.

Acceptance of this proposition does not mean that legislation based on the principles of deterrence is exempt from criticism. The basis for the criticism, however, must derive from a different source. Such criticism could be based on a deterministic view of human life. If every act is the product of heredity and environment, the choice between conforming to the law and breaking it is somewhat illusory. To say that a person *could* have acted differently is merely to state in another way that *if* he had possessed a different personality, or *if* the external situation had been different, the action, too, would have been different. The person makes a choice, to be sure, but with this given personality in this given situation, the choice could only be what it was. The Swedish law professor Vilhelm Lundstedt, one of the best known proponents of general prevention, considered punishment a necessary means to inculcate moral standards in the populace; but recognizing the force of the deterministic position, he characterized the convicted offender as "a kind of martyr to the maintenance of the social order." [10]

I do not intend to discuss the free will problem, which easily leads to a tangle of metaphysics and semantics.[11] Suffice it to say that in practical life we all tend to differentiate between those who can and those who cannot control their actions and that it is a generally accepted proposition that every normal person has to face the moral and legal responsibility for his voluntary acts. On the other hand, many thoughtful men feel a certain ambivalence, a lurking doubt, towards the concepts of guilt and responsibility. The tendency of the modern, enlightened mind to look for the individual and social causes of the criminal act makes moral indignation evaporate and may even turn it into compassion and pity. At the very least there is a feeling that many of the persons who break the law and consequently are subjected to prosecution and punishment were poorly equipped to resist the temptation. Without moral indignation, punishment is inflicted only reluctantly. For this reason, Bittner and Platt are right when they assert that the execution of punishment has become less and less compatible with prevailing moral sentiment [12]—prevailing, that is, among the well-educated and liberal-minded. As a Norwegian Supreme Court judge once said: "Our grandparents punished, and they did it with a clear conscience. We punish too, but we do it with a bad conscience." Although the institution of punishment is necessary, it is a sad necessity.

As long as legislation is restricted to achieving deterrence through economic sanctions, few people will find any moral objection. The same holds true for the threat of losing one's driver's license as a deterrent to traffic offenses. The morality of deterrence can be reasonably discussed only in relation to penalties which inflict a serious suffering, humiliation, or degradation on the offender.

The question has been most thoroughly explored in the context of the death penalty imposed for murder. Some defend the death penalty on retributive grounds irrespective of its deterrent value. Others accept it on utilitarian grounds, because they believe that the supreme penalty has a substantial deterrent effect. Of the opponents, many take the position that they will oppose capital punishment as long as it is not proven to have a more substantial deterrent effect than other forms of punishment. Others take the more absolute moral position asserting that the death penalty is unjustifiable regardless of its effect. For example, in 1902, a member of the Norwegian parliament stated during the debates on the new Penal Code: "Even if it were so that capital punishment were necessary to deter people, I cannot accept it. I cannot accept it because it runs counter to the moral principles a society ought to be built upon." [13]

In our society there would be widespread agreement that the death penalty ought not be imposed for minor offenses, and the same feeling is expressed toward long prison terms which are considered too harsh for the offense for which they are imposed. A threat of punishment which would be considered justifiable for the hijacking of an airliner would be considered excessive for car theft or shoplifting. In 1969, a twenty-year-old Virginia student without a previous criminal record was sentenced to twenty-five years in prison (with five years suspended for good behavior) for the possession of marijuana.[14] In Virginia the minimum penalty for possession of more than twenty-five grains (about half a teaspoonful) of marijuana is twenty years, the same minimum penalty as for first degree murder. This is a clear example of a punishment which is excessive in relation to the nature of the crime.

Thus, the decisive point does not seem to be whether the law is based on considerations of deterrence, but rather whether it can be accepted as a *reasonable means* to a *legitimate end*. The German courts have declared that the constitutional principle of the dignity of man requires (1) that only culpable offenders be punished, and (2) that the punishment be in just proportion to the gravity of the offense and the culpability of the offender.[15] The first restriction rules out strict liability and vicarious liability in criminal law. I shall not discuss these problems but will deal only with the second proposition.

Punishment in relation to the gravity of the offense and the culpability of the offender provides an elastic formula. Opinions as to the gravity of the offense and the culpability of the offender may differ, but the formula seems to express the essence of the common sense of justice. The formula is valid also with regard to penalties imposed on the basis of considerations other than general deterrence. The Norwegian Penal Code has a provision which prescribes a minimum penalty of two years imprisonment for aggravated larceny, provided the defendant has had at least three previous convictions for that crime.

The motivation behind this provision was a desire to insure a more efficient treatment of professional thieves. However, from time to time cases have arisen where the two-year minimum has been applied to petty thieves who happen to have committed a burglary to obtain small quantities of food. Such cases have provoked strong criticism because of the lack of proportion between crime and punishment. The legislature responded to this criticism with a 1967 amendment to the Penal Code providing that the court can disregard the minimum sentence if special circumstances are present.

Where the probability of detection of criminal behavior is low, legislatures are sometimes inclined to compensate by increasing the severity of penalties. In the history of criminal law this has been a recurrent theme. The brutality of penal law in former times is more easily understood when one considers the weakness of state organization and the absence of an organized police force.[16] No doubt a moderate level of penal sanctions combined with widespread and effective enforcement is more acceptable to the moral sentiment than harsh penalties with only sporadic enforcement. Compensating for weak enforcement with harsh penalties may also lead to severe treatment of one type of offense in relation to another offense which, although more reprehensible, is more easily detected. Such discrepancies may be justifiable from a utilitarian point of view, but they are objectionable from a retributive point of view, and if the discrepancies are glaring they might violate the widely accepted principle of reasonable proportion between crime and punishment.

CONSIDERATIONS OF GENERAL PREVENTION IN SENTENCING

The preceding discussion has been concerned solely with situations where a sentence based on considerations of deterrence is prescribed by the legislature, as when a penal provision prescribes a fixed sentence (for example, imprisonment for life for murder) or a minimum penalty binding on the courts (as in the original version of the Norwegian aggravated larceny law). However, this is seldom the prevailing pattern in modern legislation. Typically the law gives the judge broad discretion to make the sentence fit the offense and the offender. The relationship between the threat of sanction and the application of punishment thus becomes more complex. The role of the court is not only to carry out the prescriptions of the law but also to exercise its own judgment. The law could, of course, require that the judge consider only the rehabilitation of the individual offender in sentencing. In such a system, a murderer might receive a suspended sentence or probation if the judge determines that there is no danger of recidivism, and, in contrast, the petty but incorrigible thief might be imprisoned for life. But most criminal codes leave the task of weighing the different purposes of punishment, including general prevention, to the judge. For example, the Norwegian Penal Code states in section 52 that the court may suspend the punishment "unless the concern for general law-abidance or for restraining the convict from further offenses requires execution of the punishment." The "concern for general law-abidance" is meant to cover the general-preventive aspects of punishment.

In practice, it seems that judges in all countries give weight to general-preventive considerations as long as the penalty remains reasonably proportionate to the crime. For a meaningful discussion of the moral aspect of the consideration of general prevention in sentencing, it is necessary to distinguish between different situations. The court, in meting out the penalty, may consider the potential deterrent effect of *each particular sentence*. Or the court may consider the foreseeable effects of *this level of punishment for this type of offense.* Both types of considerations may be applied in the same case, and it is not easy to draw a clear line between them. Nevertheless, the distinction is important for analysis.

If the sentencing judge wishes to attach weight to the general-preventive effect of a particular sentence, he should consider the publicity which the decision will receive and the possible reactions of those people who will hear or read about the decision. If a case has for some reason attracted great publicity, a severe sentence could be expected to have great deterrent effect. If, on the other hand, the publicity is minimal, and the sentence probably will be known only to the defendant himself and the officials involved with the case, the judge could let the offender off with a light sentence without sacrificing any general-preventive effects. In a system of this kind it is a fair generalization that the offender is used as a means for the public good, and most people would find the system unjust because it would violate the principle of equality before the law. It may, to be sure, often be difficult to determine what equality means, or, in other words, what differences between two similar cases justify a different treatment, but few would disagree that differences in the amount of publicity ought to be irrelevant. For this reason, the system might also be self-defeating since a system of criminal justice which is exposed as capricious and unjust will be unable to act as an educative force. I shall not go so far as to assert that it is unjust under all circumstances to attach weight in sentencing to the deterrent effects of the particular sentence, but at least we are in an area which demands extreme caution.

The situation is different when general prevention is taken into consideration in determining the general level of penalties for different types of offenses. This seems to me both legitimate and necessary. If the Penal Code gives the court freedom to determine the sentence (for example, within the limits of one year and twenty years of imprisonment), this means that the legislature has abstained from developing a fixed and detailed system of penalties. The threat of the law has a certain indefiniteness, and the task of specifying the exact extent of the threat falls to the courts. In countries with efficient judicial review of sentencing, the supreme court establishes guidelines for the lower courts. In systems where sentencing is viewed as the exclusive, or almost exclusive, province of the trial court, the discrepancies between these courts will necessarily be greater. But in relation to the legislative enactment the task is, in principle, the same. The sentencing is simply a continuation of the evaluations begun by the legislature; and it would be arbitrary and contrary to the public interest to exclude motivations of general prevention.

What of the Kantian principle in this case? When the structure of penalties is fixed by the legislature it could not reasonably be said that the individual offender serves as a means to deter others. I tend to see it the same way when the level of penalties is fixed by the courts. But whether one agrees with these propositions is of little consequence for the moral judgment.

I shall illustrate the use of general-preventive considerations in sentencing by some cases from the Norwegian Supreme Court, chosen somewhat randomly. The Court has power to alter sanctions on lawbreakers, on appeal by the prosecutor or the defendant, and it states its reasons for doing so.

1. *1947 Norsk Retstidende 368.* A Norwegian guard in a German camp in Norway for Yugoslavian prisoners had, at the instigation of a superior, brutally killed a prisoner. The trial court sentenced the defendant to death, and the Supreme Court upheld the sentence. Justice Skau for the majority declared: "Public international law has strict rules for the treatment of prisoners of war and

accepts the highest penalties for serious crimes against them. Prisoners of war, civil as well as military, are in an especially vulnerable position and have no other defense than that which a strong legal protection can give. But a strong legal protection in this relationship supposes not only strict rules of law but also strict enforcement." Chief Justice Stang added: "As conditions have been under this war and may become under a new one it is necessary that guards and supervisors in prisons and concentration camps [learn] that to maltreat or kill a prisoner is a crime which will be severely punished. For general-preventive reasons it is therefore necessary to apply the ultimate penalty of the law."

2. *1947 Norsk Retstidende 271.* This case concerned the question of drunken driving. The law has a fixed limit of blood alcohol content (0.05 percent) and for general-preventive reasons the courts have established a practice of not suspending sentences in such cases in the absence of extraordinary circumstances. Sometimes the trial court, consisting of one judge and two lay assessors, suspends the prison sentence out of pity for the defendant. In this case the lay assessors outvoted the judge and suspended a twenty-one day prison sentence. They argued that this case was an isolated instance of drunken driving by an otherwise law-abiding citizen. On appeal by the prosecution the Supreme Court imposed a thirty-day prison sentence without suspension. The Court emphasized the great danger represented by drunken drivers and the increasing number of such drivers.

3. *1947 Norsk Retstidende 269.* The defendant, a thirty-year-old man with no previous record, had been drunk in a public place and struck a policeman. In the trial court the lay assessors, outvoting the judge, suspended a thirty-day sentence. On appeal by the prosecution the Supreme Court reversed. Judge Gaarder spoke for the court: "I find the appeal justified and, in accord with the

previous practice of this court in similar cases, the penalty should be reinstated. Considerations of general prevention speak against suspending the penalty in this type of case."

4. *1953 Norsk Retstidende 1312*. The defendant was the captain of a Bristol trawler that had been fishing illegally in Norwegian territorial waters. The trial court imposed the harshest sentence ever meted out for this offense. The captain's appeal was unsuccessful. Judge Thrap, speaking for the majority, stated that the purpose of the law forbidding trawling was to protect the vital interests of the coastal population. Illegal fishing by Norwegian and foreign trawlers caused the coastal population considerable loss and inconvenience. The trawling not only adversely affected local fishing interests, but also endangered their fishing tackle. Judge Thrap pointed out that the law had time and again been made more rigorous, and he quoted official statements regarding the need for stringent sanctions. In conclusion he stated: "Because of the strong, general-preventive considerations in this field, I take as my starting point that fines and confiscations shall be in amounts which, in each individual case, are adequate for efficient enforcement of the law." Experience had shown that the previous penalties had been insufficient. Under these circumstances, the Supreme Court saw no reason to reduce the sentence imposed by the trial court. One judge dissented. He agreed that it was justifiable to introduce stricter penalties, but was unwilling to go as far as the majority because he felt that the resulting sanction would vary too much from previous practice.

As these cases show, the Court is concerned not with the effect of the individual sentence, but rather with the effect of varying penalties for different types of offenders. It seems difficult to find valid objections to a judge taking deterrence into consideration in the same manner as a legislator does. However, we may sometimes question the beliefs of the courts with regard to the effects of a certain sentencing policy. For example, is it realistic to assume that the war crime sentences imposed in Norway after World War II will have any deterrent effect in a future wartime situation? There may also be differences in value judgments. With regard to the drunken driving cases we may ask: How many prison sentences are we willing to accept in order to save one life or save one person from crippling injury? Similar questions confront the legislature.

Considerations of general prevention are frequently mentioned by a court in deciding whether to suspend a sentence. While principles of general deterrence seem to weigh against suspension, special circumstances of the specific case may warrant suspension of sentence. For example, in the drunken driving cases the court may be motivated to suspend the sentence because of the bad health of the offender; [17] the suicidal tendencies of the offender's wife; [18] or by the lapse of time since the act was committed.[19]

Questions may arise as to which circumstances can properly be considered in determining the extent of the penalties. The next two cases serve as examples.

5. *1962 Norsk Retstidende 517*. The defendant, a nineteen-year-old man, followed an elderly woman and snatched her bag containing 750 kroner (about $100). He had no previous convictions and the trial court imposed a ninety-day suspended sentence. On appeal by the prosecution, the Supreme Court reduced the sentence to forty-five days but denied suspension. Speaking for the Court, Judge Bendiksby stated: "The prosecution has produced evidence that recently there has been a great increase in 'bag-snatching.' Since September 25, 1961, there have been eighteen cases in Oslo. The victims, according to a list which was produced in the case, are generally elderly women; the victim in this case was eighty years old. Crimes of this kind are difficult for the police to solve; in only four of the eighteen cases has the offender been

found. There is obviously a strong need to support effectively the work of the police who are trying to protect citizens who are especially exposed to this kind of attack and who have little capacity to defend themselves. When the culprit is caught, the sanction ought to be severe. I therefore find that considerations of general deterrence weigh heavily in favor of denying suspension in this type of crime."

6. *1969 Norsk Retstidende 1048.* On several occasions, the defendant, an eighteen-year-old boy, had purchased moderate quantities of hashish, sometimes with friends as partners. The trial court stated that he had actively taken part in creating a milieu of narcotics in his home town. The court imposed a sixty-day prison sentence, the last thirty-five of which were suspended. On appeal the defendant sought to have the entire sentence suspended, arguing that he was now engaged in vocational training and had broken with the narcotics milieu. Speaking for the majority, Judge Boelviken conceded that it was unnecessary to require the defendant to serve the sentence in order to prevent him from further criminal activity. However, referring to general-preventive considerations and the Court's previous practice in such cases, she held that the defendant's crime was sufficiently serious to require him to serve at least part of his sentence. Judge Hiorthöy, dissenting, believed that since the defendant bought and imported hashish only for personal use, rather than being a professional narcotics importer, principles of general deterrence should not be decisive. He felt that considerations of general deterrence should give way when imprisonment would have greatly adverse effects on the defendant. After discussing the particular circumstances of the defendant, he added that he did not feel bound by the previous rigorous practice of the Court in narcotics cases: "Conditions have changed, and the recommendation of the prosecution as well as the sentence of the court below shows that a dif-

ferent and milder course of sentencing is now followed in cases in which the defendant made only personal use of the narcotics. Such a policy expresses a view, which I share, that the general deterrent effects of punishment are questionable in relation to personal use of marijuana (hashish), and that this ought to be taken into consideration when determining whether a sentence should be suspended."

The other three judges agreed with Judge Boelviken, adding that it would be contrary to previous practice of the Court to suspend the entire sentence, and that conditions had not changed so as to justify changing that practice.

The bag-snatching case presents the question whether it is ethically defensible to increase the penalty because of changes in the crime rate or in other social conditions. I agree with the court's affirmative answer to this question. Just as the legislature considers social conditions in legislating against certain conduct, the court should have the power to adjust sentencing policy to the changing needs of society. Such adjustment may lead to less severe sentences for some crimes and to harsher sentences in others. This was the argument of the dissenting judge in the hashish case. Infanticide is an example of a crime for which there has been mitigation of former harsh sentencing practices. Since this crime no longer represents a frequent problem in the Scandinavian countries, penal sanctions for it have become much more lenient, and in the few cases which have recently been heard, the sentence has almost always been suspended.

Perhaps one exception, illustrated by a German case from the Nazi era,[20] should be made regarding the factors which the court should consider when determining a penalty. The defendant was convicted of violating a law which prohibited sexual intercourse between people of Jewish and "Aryan" nationality. The Supreme Court considered it proper to take notice that the number of such violations had greatly increased *after the commission of the act of the defendant.* While the character of the charge makes this decision especially repugnant, it seems that in any case subsequent developments should be excluded as an aggravating factor in sentencing. However, this problem will rarely arise.[21]

In Norway, the question has recently arisen as to whether it is unjust to establish two levels of sentences: one for Norwegians and a different one for foreigners. Norway is a small, peaceful country with a modest crime rate. Compared to those of other nations, punishments are mild, with few prison sentences of more than two or three years. Recently there have been several cases in which foreign, professional criminals have taken advantage of Norway's relatively mild law enforcement to engage in armed robbery, check forgery, and narcotics smuggling. Thus, the Norwegian legal system must deal with professional criminals who are accustomed to much more severe penalties in countries in which they have previously operated. It is against national interests to make Norway a tempting base for international narcotics dealers or other professional criminals drawn there by the mild criminal penalties. On the other hand, there is no wish to change the present penalties imposed on Norwegian citizens. Nevertheless, such a dual system seems objectionable, especially when a Norwegian and a foreign national are involved in the same crime.

Sentencing practices vary from one country to another; for example, sentencing in the Scandinavian countries differs in many respects from that in the United States. With the exception of penalties for drunken driving, sentencing in the Scandinavian countries is much more uniform and more lenient. It is therefore dangerous to generalize. A study of sentencing practice in Norway leads to the conclusion that when general deterrence considerations are part of the grounds of a judgment, the general penalty level, not the effect of the particular sentence, is determinative. However, this is not necessarily the case in other countries.

Nigel Walker's exposition on "exemplary sentences," for example, seemingly reveals a willingness of English courts to adjust a sentence to the needs of deterrence felt in the particular case. "A judge who believes that more severe sentences will influence potential offenders, but who cannot ensure that his colleagues will adopt his policy, will sometimes impose sentences which are markedly more severe than the norm for the express purpose of increasing their deterrent effect." [22] Exemplary sentences, Walker explains, are usually imposed to deal with a specific offense which has suddenly become more frequent or which has attracted much publicity, especially if the instances of the offense are limited to a certain locality.

A famous example of this system at work is the use of harsh sentences to suppress attacks on blacks in the Nottinghill district of London in 1958.[23] Nine boys, six only seventeen years old and all but one with no police record, were sentenced to four years imprisonment. This imposition of exemplary sentences was upheld by the Court of Criminal Appeal. Other trials followed, in which offenders received lighter sentences; and the race riots waned after the exemplary sentences. But it is extremely difficult to ascertain the role of the exemplary sentences in ending the turmoil.

Walker supports using criminal penalties as a deterrent but argues against the occasional exemplary sentence, not for ethical reasons but because he questions the effectiveness of the exemplary sentence. However, there may be fields where the exemplary sentence works effectively; white collar crime may be such a field. A high official of the Antitrust Division of the United States Justice Department stated some years ago:

No one in direct contact with the living reality of business conduct in the United States is unaware of the effect the imprisonment of seven high officials in the electrical Machinery Industry in 1960 had on the conspiratorial price fixing in many areas of our economy; similar sentences in a few cases each decade would almost completely cleanse our economy of the cancer of collusive price fixing and the mere prospect of such sentences is itself the strongest available deterrent to such activities.[24]

Even assuming that unusually heavy penalties of the Nottinghill type have the desired effect, such penalties may be objectionable from an ethical standpoint because they are arbitrary, imposing unequal treatment on one actor compared to another who may be equally blameworthy. But it will not always be easy to tell whether an exemplary sentence is being imposed. As mentioned above, the distinction between the two points at which considerations of general prevention can enter the sentencing process (in calculating the effects of a certain *level of penalties* or of a *particular sentence*) is not a sharp one. A judge in deciding the right level of penalties for a specific crime at a specific time and place comes close to considering the effects of the particular sentence. And it may happen that the judge, in pronouncing a sentence harsher than previous practice would dictate, does not himself know whether he is changing to a new level of penalties or only temporarily parting from the standard sentence to impose an exemplary sentence.

Sometimes it may seem fictitious to talk about determining a level of sentencing, because the case under consideration is more or less unique. The *Quisling* case may serve as an example. The Norwegian Supreme Court sentenced Quisling to death for treason, apparently motivated by a belief that it was necessary to apply the supreme penalty for reasons of general prevention.[25] If it is granted that the death penalty is permissible, the decision is not objectionable. There is no disproportion between crime and punishment and no breach of the principle of equality before the law.

Proof of Deterrent Effect

The result of our discussion so far can be summed up in this statement: Punishment on the basis of general prevention is ethically defensible, both in legislation and sentencing, if the penalty is in reasonable proportion to the gravity of the offense and does not violate the principle of equality before the law. However, the question may be raised from another angle. It is often asserted that there is no scientific proof for the general-preventive effects of punishment, and it may be argued that it is morally unjustifiable to inflict punishment on the basis of a belief which is not corroborated by scientific evidence. The burden of proof, it is sometimes said, is on those who would invoke punishment. Others may answer that the burden of proof is on those who would experiment at the risk of society by removing or weakening the protection which the criminal law now provides.

Two points should be made. First, our lack of knowledge of general prevention may be exaggerated. In some areas of criminal law we have experiences which come as close to scientific proof as could be expected in human affairs. In many other areas it seems reasonably safe to evaluate the general-preventive effects of punishment on a common sense basis. Modern psychology has shown that the pleasure–pain principle is not as universally valid as is assumed, for instance, in Bentham's penal philosophy. Nevertheless, it is still a fundamental fact of social life that the risk of unpleasant consequences is a very strong motivational factor for most people in most situations.

Second, even in questions of social and economic policy we rarely are able to base our decisions on anything which comes close to strict scientific proof. Generally we must act on the basis of our best judgment. In this respect, the problems of penal policy are the same as problems of education, housing, foreign trade policy, and so on. The development of social science gradually provides a better factual foundation for decisions of social policy, but there is a long way to go. Besides, research always lags behind the rapid change of social conditions.

However, it is undeniable that punishment—the intentional infliction of suffering—is a special category among social policies. It contrasts sharply with the social welfare measures which characterize our modern state. This calls for caution and moderation in its application. I do not think the legal concept of "burden of proof" is very useful in this context. The balance that should be struck between defense of society and humaneness towards the offender can hardly be expressed in a simple formula. The solution of the conflict will depend on individual attitudes. Some people identify more with the values threatened by criminal behavior; others identify more with the lawbreaker. But certainly punishment should not be imposed precipitously. History provides a multitude of examples of shocking cruelty based on ideas of deterrence, often in combination with ideas of just retribution.

One conclusion ought to be beyond controversy. As long as society feels obliged to use punishment for general-preventive reasons, it is important for researchers to attempt to evaluate the accuracy of the assumptions that lawmakers, courts, and law enforcement agencies make about general prevention. This is a badly neglected field of research. It may be necessary and ethically justifiable to base policy decisions on common sense reasoning, often amounting to sheer guesswork, as long as no other alternative exists. But it is morally indefensible to continue to punish other human beings without making real efforts to replace speculation with scientific facts.

Notes

1. Hawkins, *Punishment and Deterrence: The Educative, Moralizing, and Habituative Effects,* 1969 WIS. L. REV. 550; see also chapter 2, pp. 35–36, and *Appendix 1.*
2. Bittner & Platt, *The Meaning of Punishment,* 2 ISSUES IN CRIMINOLOGY 79, 93 (1966).
3. Kant, *Metaphysische Anfangsgründe der Rechtslehre,* zweiter Teil, erster Abschnitt, DAS STAATSRECHT ALLGEMEINE ANMERKUNG E. (1797). The question has been thoroughly discussed in German literature since World War II as a reaction to the extreme application of general deterrence under the Nazi regime. See Bruns, *Die "Generalpraevention" als Zweck und Zumessungsgrund der Strafe?,* FESTSCHRIFT FÜR HELLMUT VON WEBER ZUM 70. GEBURTSTAG (1963). Several authors have expressed the opinion that the acceptance of general prevention as an aim of punishment violates article 1 of the new German Constitution, which declares the dignity of man inviolable. Some also adduce the European Convention of Human Rights in support of their position. The German courts, however, have not accepted these views. See 1968 DEUTSCHE JURISTENZEITUNG 388; Judgment of May 6, 1954, 6 Entscheidungen des Bundesgerichtshofs in Strafsachen [BGHSt.] 125; Judgment of Aug. 4, 1965, 20 BGHSt. 264.
4. It should be noted in passing that the other traditional justifications for punishment are also subject to attack. Retribution as a goal of criminal justice is generally condemned by modern authors. And reform and rehabilitation, long the goals of reformers, have been increasingly criticized in recent years. Experience has shown how even the best of intentions can lead to oppressive results. Thus, efforts at reform and rehabilitation, according to critics, should not exceed the limits established by the other purposes of punishment. Norval Morris, for instance, states as a leading principle of criminal policy: *"Power over a criminal's life should not be taken in excess of that which would be taken were his reform not con-*

sidered as one of our purposes. The maximum of his punishment should never be greater than that which would be justified by the other aims of our criminal justice." Morris, *Impediments to Penal Reform,* 33 U. Chi. L. Rev. 627, 638 (1966) (emphasis in original). Restraint of dangerous offenders seems to be the only traditional justification of punishment still meeting with general approval, and this justification applies to only a small segment of offenders.

Generally the controversy over punishment reflects differences of opinion with regard to the justification of an institution considered indispensable. But there are also voices which question the institution of punishment itself. Bittner and Platt state that "while the punitive approach has, to all appearances, no future, psychologically oriented treatment is in ascendance." Bittner & Platt, *supra* note 2, at 98-99. Their explanation for this shift is that the execution of punishment has become less and less compatible with prevailing moral sentiment. "Thus, it appears that in the long run it could not possibly matter whether punishment works or not, for it has been going out of use, not gracefully, but inexorably." *Id.*

5. As quoted by Radzinowicz and Turner in *A Study on Punishment: Introductory Essay,* 21 Can. B. Rev. 91, 92 (1943).

6. We shall leave aside the problem of whether general prevention does play or ought to play a role in the execution of sentences and in decisions about release on parole.

7. Bittner & Platt, *supra* note 2, at 93.

8. Hart, Punishment and Responsibility 23 (1968).

9. Feuerbach, Revision der Grundsätze und Grundbegriffe des positiven peinlichen Rechts, erster Teil, at 48-58 (1799).

10. As quoted in 31 Svensk Juristtidning 373 (1946).

11. A detailed analysis of the problem is given in Ofstad, An Inquiry into the Freedom of Decision (1961). For a brief discussion see Andenaes, *Determinism and Criminal Law,* 47 J. Crim. L.C. & P.S. 406 (1956).

12. Bittner & Platt, *supra* note 2.

13. 1902 Odelstingsforhandlinger 438.

14. Life, Nov. 10, 1969, at 24.

15. 1968 Deutsche Juristenzeitung 388.

16. See Schmidt, Einfuehrung in die Geschichte der deutschen Strafrechtspflege 63-64, 93-94 (2d ed. 1951); Radzinowicz, A History of English Criminal Law, Vol. 1 (1948); Anners, Humanitet och rationalism 14-15 (1965).

17. 1968 Norsk Retstidende 737.

18. *Id.* at 705.

19. *Id.* at 707.

20. 1937 Juristische Wochenschrift 3083.

21. In the Norwegian bag-snatching case cited above, it is not clear from the judgment whether the Court made any distinction according to whether the change in the crime rate had taken place before or after the commission of the crime.

22. Walker, Sentencing in a Rational Society 68–69 (1969).

23. *Id.* at 69–70; Wootton, Crime and the Criminal Law 100–101 (1963); see also chapter 2, pp. 39, 78.

24. Spivack, as quoted in Cressey & Ward, Delinquency, Crime, and Social Process 210 (1969).

25. 1945 Norsk Retstidende 109 (quoted in chapter 2, p. 39).

VI

THE FUTURE OF CRIMINAL LAW

My home city, Oslo (or, as it was then called, Kristiania) witnessed a rapid expansion in the 1890's. To meet the demands on the traffic system which the future would bring, the board of the City Streetcar Company is said to have drawn up a thirty-year plan for the development of the company. This was in the time of horse-drawn street-cars, and the plan computed the numbers of cars and horses, stables, and storage space for hay and other fodder which would be needed in the 1920's. When the 1920's arrived, of course, no horses, no stables, and no storage space for fodder were needed.

On a small scale, this local story, the truth of which I am not prepared to guarantee, illustrates the enormous difficulties in making long-term forecasts. The subject which we have come to call futurology is a fascinating intellectual exercise, but full of pitfalls. Let us imagine that prior to World War I, a team of the best available experts in history, science, sociology, and so forth had been given the task of forecasting the trends of the next fifty years. They would have been able to foresee scientific and technical advances—but how could they possibly have foreseen the really decisive and unique events to come: World War I, the Russian Revolution, the rise of Fascism and Nazism, the Stalin terror, World War II, the nuclear bomb, the cold war, the emergence of the new China, the hippie movement and student unrest, just to mention a few?

Every forecast of future development has to be based on certain assumptions which are taken for granted. The validity of the forecast is dependent on the soundness of the premises. If the basis proves inadequate the forecast cannot claim to be valid. This chapter is limited to societies of the Western type, and will start from the basic assumptions of a reasonably peaceful development within the framework of a democratic political structure, and of continued economic growth and continued expansion of social welfare without fundamental changes in the social system. I do not assume that this development in itself will make the crime rate dwindle, and thus render the problems of crime and criminal law less urgent. Experience up to now warrants no such optimism.

Having thus stated my points of departure I am left with at least two pitfalls. The first is the danger of an uncritical prolongation of present trends. We know from history that one trend may supersede another, but standing in the stream of events it is difficult to obtain an adequate perspective. The second is the danger of projecting one's own wishes into the future. There is a natural tendency to assume that the future will reveal how right one is, and therefore will move in the direction one feels would be right. I do not feel confident that I have avoided either of these dangers.

THE END OF PUNISHMENT?

The first question which immediately arises is: Does criminal law have a future at all? That is, criminal law in the traditional meaning as a body of law regulating the conditions of punishment and the choice of penalty. Many reformers consider the abolition of punishment not a

Utopian ideal but the inevitable result of present development. The famous American psychiatrist Karl Menninger, in his well-known book *The Crime of Punishment,* characterizes our criminal law as "a social monstrosity." He speaks of "our present stupid, futile, abominable practice against detected offenders." And the American criminologists Bittner and Platt, less emotionally but no less confidently, assert that "in the long run it could not possibly matter whether punishment works or not, for it has been going out of use, not gracefully, but inexorably." This is so, they feel, because punishment has become less and less compatible with prevailing moral sentiment.[1] The list of similar statements could easily be extended.

I feel these voices express some fundamental change in moral sentiment. In our Western world punishment has become far less acceptable than it was some generations ago, not only in criminal justice; we can discover this attitude in many walks of life. Parents feel guilty if they chastise their child; in schools and public institutions the use of punishment has been very greatly reduced; in religious teaching the idea of doom and eternal suffering, which was accepted dogma some generations ago, has practically disappeared. The reasons for this dwindling popularity of punishment may be complex. Part of the explanation certainly lies in the development of psychology and psychiatry; representatives of these sciences have effectively propagated other methods of education and treatment. Moreover, the scientific outlook of the present age, with its concentration of interest on the individual and social causes of deviant behavior, has undermined belief in punishment as the just desert for evil-doing. Whatever the reasons, the fact is undeniable. A hundred years ago, good Christians felt no qualms about the idea of a merciful God condemning the wicked to eternal suffering in Hell. Good people were supposed to enjoy eternal bliss in Heaven, without being disturbed by the thought of the wicked undergoing indescribable and never-ending sufferings in the nether regions. Modern sentiment has found this idea intolerable and repulsive. Even though the idea of Hell has not been formally renounced by the Church it is passed over in silence.[2]

Because of this emotional background I expect that there will be a closer scrutiny of the need for punishment in the future, a greater cost-awareness in the use of the criminal sanction. This refers both to the extent of criminalization and to the seriousness of the sanction. My predecessor in the chair of criminal law at the University of Oslo said in his textbook on the subject that, having studied the history of criminal law, one might be tempted to conclude that the most numerous and grossest ill-deeds have been committed by public authorities in the name of justice.[3] When I read this as a young man I felt it must be a great exaggeration. Now I am inclined to think he was right. We have gone a long way towards mitigating the system and removing offenses from the statute book. This development will probably continue, and would be possible within the present structure of criminal law. But more radical changes are perfectly conceivable.

PUNISHMENT AND TREATMENT

While punishment has come to sound somewhat brutal and old-fashioned, treatment and rehabilitation of the offender sounds enlightened and humane. It is, therefore, no wonder that the substitution of treatment for punishment has come to be looked upon as the goal for the future.

The most radical reformers envisage the whole system of criminal justice transformed into a system of treatment, based exclusively on the need for rehabilitating the offender or, if this appears impossible, detaining him as long as necessary to prevent him from doing more harm. Almost of necessity a system of this kind presupposes indeterminate sentences, leaving it to administrative authorities or some kind of treatment tribunal to decide when to release the offender.

Now, treatment is an ambiguous term. To some reformers it signifies the application of the technical skill of psychiatrists, psychologists, and other treatment personnel in dealing with personality disorders, as contrasted with traditional penal methods. Others interpret the term in a wider sense, so as to comprise as well methods used in more traditional prison work, with deprivation of liberty and work training as the main components.

Even when treatment is interpreted in this broader sense I do not believe in the vision of a system based exclusively on treatment of the individual offender. I consider the idea suffers from an underestimation of the general deterrent function of criminal law, and even more important, from an overestimation of our ability to treat and predict criminal behavior. Before enlarging upon this I should like to approach the problem in a somewhat theoretical way, looking at the *legal technique* applied in criminal law as compared with legislation on health and social welfare.

The technique of criminal law, as Professor Hart emphasizes, consists primarily in announcing certain standards of conduct and attaching unpleasant consequences to acts (or omissions) violating those standards, thereby hoping to motivate people to conform.[4] The primary purpose of criminal law is to act as a threat; the primary purpose of enforcement and punishment is to make the threat credible. In the past, the law itself specified the penalty for breach of the law; this task, within certain limits, is now entrusted to the judge, thus making the system more flexible.

Legislation in the field of health and social welfare has a fundamentally different approach. In the first place, such legislation is primarily concerned with establishing *offers* to the clients, with giving them opportunities for treatment or other social benefits. Second, when compulsory measures are called for, the clients are not described with reference to particular acts they have committed, but with reference to their *status* as suffering from illness, as being in need of care and treatment, or as representing a danger to others. The provisions of such legislation are not intended to act as threats, although they may in fact be so conceived by some of the clients.

There are admittedly hybrid forms of legislation, and we are not always very happy about them. I am thinking of such phenomena as vagrancy legislation, juvenile delinquency legislation, or American statutes authorizing civil commitment for sexual psychopaths.

The idea of transforming the whole system of criminal justice into a system of individualized treatment would mean a radical fusion of hitherto separate branches of law. The detailed definitions of offenses, if they were to be retained at all, would become descriptions of symptoms characteristic of persons who need treatment or require incapacitation.

Let me give some reasons why I consider such a development highly unlikely.

1. My first point concerns the great bulk of offenses which fall outside the borders of traditional crime but which, in modern society, have gained an ever increasing importance. One major group consists of traffic offenses, from dangerous driving and driving under the influence of alcohol to the most trivial parking offense. Another group, which has come to be known as public welfare offenses, comprises violations of all kinds of economic regulations. It is fairly obvious that a system of individual treatment for offenders in these fields is neither possible nor called for. It has been proposed to remove these kinds of offenses from the sphere of criminal law proper by not calling the sanction concerned a criminal sanction. "Minor traffic

offenses, violation of food and drug laws, building-code infractions, and the like," says Packer, "are best dealt with through the agency of the civil rather than the criminal law." [5] Terms such as "civil offense," "infraction," and "violation" have been variously proposed for this category. I do not intend to discuss these proposals. Suffice it to say that, whatever the name of the sanction and the mode of procedure, the technique involved is one that is typical of criminal law.

2. At the other end of the scale, there is a range of serious crimes, which call for severe sanctions on grounds of general deterrence, even when the individual offender is in no need of treatment and represents no danger, or at least no danger which could not be met by other means. By way of illustration I might mention espionage, murder, large-scale trading in narcotics, hijacking of airliners, and kidnapping.

3. What the spokesmen of a treatment system probably have in mind are the more common types of traditional crime, especially property crimes, sex crimes, and crimes of violence. But even in this field we encounter enormous difficulties in putting a treatment ideology into practice.

During the last two decades criminological research has demonstrated how little we understand of the problem of curing criminals. We know that the majority of convicted first offenders are not reconvicted, and that the risk of reconviction increases with every new conviction. But it seems to make little difference to the reconviction rate which sanction we apply.[6] Whether an offender is fined, put on probation, or gets a prison sentence does not seem to matter much; likewise, the success rate seems to be about the same whether he gets an indeterminate sentence or a sentence of only a few months, and whether he is locked up in an old-fashioned prison or serves his time in an open institution. It looks as if our choice of sanction has very little effect compared with the personality and back-ground of the offender and the social environment he re-turns to after his encounter with the machinery of justice.

It is true that research into the efficacy of various treat-ments has been concerned only with the *overall* results of different treatments on comparable groups of offenders. It is theoretically possible that treatment *A* works best for one personality type, treatment *B* for another, and treat-ment *C* for a third, and that these differences neutralize each other when we compute the total success rate. We should not abandon the hope that progress will be made in relating the kind of treatment to the type of offender. But the prospects seem slim. My personal feeling is that re-search into the comparative effects of various sanctions has dealt a devastating blow to the treatment optimism many of us indulged in twenty or thirty years ago. No other fact has changed my own outlook so much.

THE INDETERMINATE SENTENCE

It follows from what I have been saying that I do not be-lieve the future lies with the indeterminate sentence. The idea of the indeterminate sentence is based on an analogy from the hospital: the patient should be kept as long as it is necessary to cure him, no shorter, no longer; and, just as with a stay in a hospital, the duration should not be decided in advance but on the basis of the observation of progress. The idea has a strong appeal; it substitutes a seem-ingly rational principle for the traditional meting out of punishment. But the difficulties of putting the principle into practice are formidable.

There are, no doubt, offenders who are psychiatric cases and whose disposition to crime may be effectively cured by psychiatric treatment. But for the great bulk of offenders the hospital analogy just does not work. We are unable to establish how the propensity to crime changes in the course of treatment, we do not know whether the chances of success will be better or worse after six months than after two or five years. Fixing the date of release on this criterion would mean that the fate of the offender would depend on the merest guesswork.

There has been a great deal of experimenting with more or less indeterminate sentences, particularly in the United States, but also in youth prison systems in England and the Scandinavian countries. Yet I know of no place where the date of release is determined solely on the basis of the hospital analogy. In the Scandinavian countries it has been found unworkable in the Borstal-style youth prisons. Instead, fairly uniform periods have been established in practice, with some consideration given to good or bad behavior and job possibilities. The American parole system uses prediction methods as an aid in determining release, but, as far as I know, the predictions are general predictions of good or bad success chances that do not take into consideration the effects which an early or late release may have. Even the comments to the American Model Penal Code, which authorizes a comprehensive scheme of fairly indeterminate sentences, admit that the available research on parole is of limited assistance in determining the time of release, since prediction studies have focused on the risk of violation if an offender is paroled rather than on the more difficult problem of *when* he should be paroled.[7]

The minor but seemingly incorrigible offender presents an embarrassing problem for any system. In a system with fixed sentences, proportional to the gravity of the offense, we face the seemingly irrational sight of men going in and out of prison until old age saps their criminal energy or ability. But in a system of indeterminate sentences the problem is no less awkward. What are we to do with the ordinary thief or burglar, who has been convicted ten times and is almost certain to come back for the eleventh?

Should we draw the conclusion that he is to be detained for a lifetime or until his criminal energy is broken by old age and the effects of prison life? For humanitarian reasons most of us will shrink from this consequence. As Packer puts it: "Incapacitation . . . is the other side of the rehabilitative coin. It may well seem a dark underside." [8]

At least in Scandinavian countries the trend in recent years has been away from sanctions of indeterminate duration back to the traditional system of fixed sentences meted out by the court. This change is not due to theoretical speculation, but to experience and research.

THE SHORT PRISON SENTENCE

A system of indeterminate sentences presupposes of necessity rather long periods of detention. Many reformers would consider this an advantage; for almost 100 years it has been considered an aim of penal reform to get away from short sentences. Such sentences do not afford the possibility of rehabilitative work with the offender, but are sufficient to brand him with the stigma of prison and to establish undesirable contacts—so the stock arguments run. And recently these ideas have made an impact on both English and German law, restricting the application of short prison sentences.

It seems to me an irony of history that these amendments should have been made precisely at a time when research has shaken the foundations of the reform movement. Research into the effects of various sanctions seems to indicate that it does not make much difference to the success rate whether the stay in prison is of shorter or longer duration. Hood and Sparks in their recent review of research findings state categorically: "Longer institutional sentences are no more effective in preventing re-

cidivism than shorter ones. Only a few studies have compared long and short sentences in the same type of institutional regime. Without exception, however, these show
that, in general, longer sentences—even of an avowedly
reformative kind—do not produce lower reconviction
rates." [9] The "without exception" is an overstatement; the
findings are not that uniform.[10] But there is certainly not
much evidence to show that the time factor is of great importance. And sociological research into the prison community and the so-called process of prisonization makes it
perfectly understandable that this should be the case. To
put it in very simple terms: the longer prison term must
have a stronger deterrent effect on the offender than the
shorter one, but this may be neutralized by the accumu-
lating negative effects of the stay in prison. Belief in the
reformative effects of prison seems, to a large extent, to
have been wishful thinking. One may have more or less
hope that a kind of therapeutic community will replace the
present prison, but even if one takes an optimistic view
in this respect it is not self-evident that a long period of
treatment will bring better results than a short one.

While it is difficult to say with any confidence that a
longer sentence will have a greater reformative effect than
a shorter one, the short sentence has at least one great advantage, namely that it is *short*. By short sentences I am
thinking mainly of those varying from a few weeks to some
months. A short sentence means less suffering for the offender and his family and less expense for society. It has two
obvious limitations; it does not effectively serve an incapacitative function, and as a general deterrent it is infer-
ior to longer sentences. There will continue to be a need
for long custodial sentences for a limited number of dangerous offenders, and there will be a need for long sentences as a deterrent to the most serious types of crime.
Organized professional crime needs special consideration
in this regard. But with these limitations borne in mind,

I see no objection to retaining the short prison sentence as the backbone of the penal system when a fine or a probation sentence is considered insufficient.[11] Fines and probation sentences have, to a great extent, come to replace prison sentences, and it is possible that this trend will continue for humanitarian and economic reasons. But these sanctions need the prison in the background as the ultimate reaction against the uncooperative.

Personally, I feel tempted to take one more step backward. The Philadelphia and Auburn systems were created to prevent the harmful effects of intimate contacts between inmates. These lessons have been forgotten, and in our time the reform movement has gone in the direction of unlimited contact possibilities. The idea has been that to train a man for life in a free society, one should make conditions in the institutions as similar as possible to the society outside. I have grave doubts about this philosophy. I believe, on common sense grounds, that the educative efforts of the prison staff are bound to have a very weak impact compared with the mutual influence of the inmates in a society of criminals. The more the prison has come to be reserved for the recidivist, the more saturated with criminal attitudes the prison community tends to become. I admit that a system of solitary confinement and *long* sentences is indefensible both from humanitarian and from mental health points of view. With *short* sentences, perhaps up to a few months, the situation is totally different. I have a great deal of sympathy for a system in which short sentences are served in solitary confinement, broken only by common activities under close supervision. This would be deterrent without being inhumane, and it would give the treatment personnel a fair possibility of coming into real contact with the inmate. But I do not believe that future development will go in the direction I would recommend. I tend to think we are faced with an irreversible process.

TOWARDS A MORALLY NEUTRAL SYSTEM
OF SANCTIONS?

I shall now turn to a somewhat less radical proposal than that of transforming the criminal law into a system of treatment pure and simple.

In the traditional system, punishment is a means of expressing social disapproval of the act. The criminal trial has been described as a "morality play," [12] and even as a degradation ceremony." [13] Conviction and sentence leave a moral stigma, the convicted person is "branded." The moral stigma may be very slight, almost nonexistent, in traffic offenses and other minor violations, or, for different reasons, in the case of conscientious objectors and other offenders whose motives are accepted as idealistic. But at least in traditional crimes the moral stigma of punishment is prominent. The character of punishment as a moral censure no doubt enhances the deterrent effect. For some groups of offenders the stigmatizing is more painful, and therefore more frightening, than the actual penalty inflicted. And criminal law is greatly concerned with punishing only the really blameworthy. The law requires a voluntary act, a guilty mind, and a responsible person. If these requirements are not met, punishment is not considered proper, although other measures of social control may be considered necessary.

There is a trend of thought which would like to abolish the distinction between punishment and other social measures, and scrap the concepts of culpability and responsibility. I call this a less radical proposal because treatment of the individual is not necessarily considered the only goal of the envisaged sanction system. It may be accepted that general deterrence has a proper place in the system beside the effects of the sanction on the individual offender, but it is argued that this does not necessitate or justify the distinctions in the present system between "sick" and "bad," between treatment and punishment. There would merely be a series of measures to choose among, whether the offender is normal or mentally sick, according to the interests of society and of the individual himself. The prison and the mental hospital would be possibilities on an equal footing, with no more moral blame or stigma attached to the one than to the other.

The first proposal of this kind was, I think, the famous Italian draft by Ferri in 1921, in which punishment and other preventive measures were jointly grouped under the term "sanctions." The Fascist dictatorship put an end to the project. The thought emerged again in the Soviet reform of the Russian Penal Code after the revolution. The Russian Penal Code of 1926 avoided the term "punishment" and spoke instead of "measures for social defence." As we all know, Soviet penal theory and legislation later swung back in the direction of guilt and punishment. In Sweden the idea of abolishing the concept of punishment was seriously discussed after World War II, but in the end the new Criminal Code of 1962 retained the term punishment and the distinction between punishment and other measures. The only code I know of which has discarded the term punishment, is the Danish Criminal Code for Greenland from 1954, which uses the neutral expression "measures" for the whole system of sanctions. But, of course, both the natural conditions and the historical tradition of Greenland are very different from Denmark and other countries in the Western world.

The psychological background to this trend of thought lies, I think, in a deterministic outlook on human life. If every act is a product of heredity and environment, the distinction between those who "could help" and those who "could not help" the act becomes somewhat dubious. If we say that a person could have acted differently, that is, from a deterministic view, only another way of stating that *if* he had been a different personality or *if* the situation had been different, the act too would have been different. In the writings of Ferri, for instance, this theoretical background of determinism is very pronounced. His first scientific contribution was his dissertation attacking the idea of free will. The same determinist attitude is characteristic of the leading Swedish reformer, Karl Schlyter, a prominent judge and former minister of justice, who was chairman of the committee whose work led to the Criminal Code of 1962. His basic idea was that we should become accustomed to looking upon the offender without reproach and moral indignation. The offender has become what he is because of innate tendencies and the influence of the environment to which he has been exposed. Society must protect itself against him, but moral reproach or indignation is just as inappropriate when applied to the responsible as when applied to those deemed irresponsible. The consequence of this view is a system of sanctions dispensing with the moral reproach which the concepts of responsibility, guilt, and punishment imply. Lady Wootton takes much the same view, although she does not find it necessary to accept a positively deterministic view. She finds it decisive that it is impossible to distingush between the "wicked" and the "sick." [14]

Will this be the approach in the future? It seems obvious that the development of criminal law will depend on the moral climate in society. No doubt our age is more concerned with the search for causes and cures, and less with moralizing, than previous periods. But even so, we are still used to thinking and speaking in terms of moral blame and moral praise, and I find it hard to believe that this will change fundamentally in the foreseeable future. As long as this is the case, conviction for an evil act will inevitably entail a moral stigma. I do not think it would make much difference if the legislature in a progressive mood decided to replace the term punishment with some more neutral-sounding term like sanction or social measure.

If conviction and punishment normally imply moral condemnation there will be a natural wish to spare those who do not seem fit objects for moral blame. It may be that as a technical reform the insanity defence could be abolished, and the state of mind of the offender be relevant only to the choice of sanction. Such is the rule under the new Swedish Code. But the Swedish Code does not go to the full extent of placing normal and insane offenders on the same footing. When the act is committed under the influence of insanity imprisonment can never be imposed. I would suppose this restriction to have strong support in public opinion. Independent of all theoretical and philosophical consideration, the idea that it is unjust, or at least inhumane, to punish the insane offender has become so entrenched in our culture that it will not easily be abandoned.

Lady Wootton has a much more radical proposal than the abolition of the insanity defence. She is in favor of abolishing the requirement of *mens rea*. Everybody who happens to have committed a prohibited act, even through no fault of his own, should be convicted, and after conviction the judge or a sentence tribunal should consider what measure, if any, should be taken. I do not regard this as a realistic alternative. It would be technically very difficult to write a criminal code on this principle, to describe, for instance, theft or fraud or criminal attempt without including a mental element in the description. And it would, in my opinion, be a very awkward system, which would mean that every motorist who had killed another would be brought to court and convicted, I suppose, of homicide, leaving it to the sentencing stage to take into consideration whether the causing of death was intentional, negligent, or a sheer and unavoidable accident. I see no social purpose served by dragging people into court and having them convicted when the police investigation has already made it clear that no blame attaches to them.

CONSERVATISM AND RADICALISM IN
CRIMINAL POLICY

To sum up, I both favor and predict a criminal law which is openly and sincerely penal in outlook and does not try to take refuge behind benevolent rhetoric about treating and rehabilitating deviants; a criminal law, that is, based primarily on general deterrence [15] and considerations of justice. This does not, of course, mean a system which considers retribution an end in itself, nor does it necessarily mean a harsh system. And it does not mean a system which neglects the aspects of treatment and rehabilitation. I am all in favor of considerable investment in efforts at treatment and rehabilitation, even though I am not too optimistic about the results, but these efforts should take place within a system where coercion and loss of liberty are primarily based on other considerations.

This seems to be a conservative view—some would no doubt feel inclined to use a stronger word. But then, what does conservative mean? In a highly perceptive lecture on "Conservative and Radical Criminal Policy in the Nordic Countries," [16] given a few years ago and now available in English, the Finnish Professor of Criminal Law, Inkeri Anttila, described as radical those who are willing to adjust criminal law rapidly to changes in social conditions and ethical evaluations, and as conservative those who are inclined to move at a slower pace and retain the existing balance until it appears obviously wrong. She goes on to say:

> I have now neglected one group: the extreme treatment supporters, who would do away with punishment in its present form and go completely over to enforced treatment of criminals. I have no room for them in my scheme. They are not conservative, as they have not yet achieved the practical political goals they might wish to

conserve. I would not call them radical either, because their retention of the traditional treatment ideology is perhaps actually related to a conservatism as far as attitudes go, perhaps an inability to accept more recent research results and adjust their own attitudes accordingly. Voluntary care is of course quite another matter.

This coincides entirely with my own views.

CRIMINAL LAW AND THE VOLUME OF CRIME

It is sometimes said that the high incidence of crime, or the rising crime rate, is evidence of the futility or impotence of the present system. Thus Lady Wootton in her book on *Crime and the Criminal Law* (p. 40) points to "the continual failure of a mainly punitive system to diminish the volume of crime." It is somewhat surprising to hear this argument from an analytic mind such as Lady Wootton's. Under any system of criminal sanctions a certain balance will be established. As long as the system remains unchanged, any changes in the amount of crime must be due to other causes. In view of developments so far, it would be more logical to reverse Lady Wootton's argument and conclude that since crime has been increasing during a period when the punitive character of the system of criminal law has been mitigated, one must assume that the system today is less effective in combating crime than the previous, harsher and more punitive system.

I do not think that crime statistics can be used as evidence in support of this, since the volume of crime is dependent on so many other and probably stronger factors, but on common sense grounds the proposition seems reasonable. The deterrent effect of the system must have been diminished by the introduction of alternative measures to prison and a milder sentencing practice. And there is little evidence that this is outweighed by greater success in treatment as a result of the wider choice of sanctions now at the disposal of the courts, and the progress that has been made in prison administration. The system has become more humane, but we cannot with any confidence assert that it yields better results. Nor is there much hope of radical progress. No breakthrough seems to be around the corner. In the treatment of psychiatric illness new drugs have changed the picture dramatically, but nothing comparable seems likely in the field of crime prevention.

But although we may suspect that our handling of the crime problem is less effective in suppressing crime than, let us say, around the turn of the century, that does not mean that one should long for a return of the old system. It is a question of values, how much weight we should attach to the suppression of crime compared to the human suffering and social cost involved. The balance has shifted in favor of the offender. This shift may continue or there may be a swing back. The criminal policy of the future will no doubt be based more on research and fact-finding than previously; it will, we hope, be less of a leap in the dark; but that does not mean that value questions will be of less importance, simply that they will have to be faced more squarely.

Notes

1. Bittner & Platt, *The Meaning of Punishment,* in: ISSUES IN CRIMINOLOGY, Vol. 2, 79 (1966).
2. MOBERLY, THE ETHICS OF PUNISHMENT 329 (1968).
3. SKEIE, DEN NORSKE STRAFFERETT, Vol. 1 15 (1937).
4. Hart, *Prolegomenon to the Principles of Punishment,* in: PUNISHMENT AND RESPONSIBILITY, 23 (1968).
5. PACKER, THE LIMITS OF THE CRIMINAL SANCTION (1968).
6. Summary of research in HOOD & SPARKS, KEY ISSUES IN CRIMINOLOGY chaps. 6 and 7 (1970).
7. MODEL PENAL CODE, TENTATIVE DRAFT NO. 5 98 (1956).
8. PACKER, *op. cit.,* 55.

9. Hood & Sparks, Key Issues in Criminology 90 (1970).
10. Hood and Sparks seem to have overlooked a Scottish study which found that sentences of six to twelve months were more effective than shorter ones; see the Scottish Advisory Council's Report on the Use of Short Sentences of Imprisonment, 1960, Appendix F. German research on young offenders has come to similar conclusions (survey by Schaffstein in Kriminologische Gegenwartsfragen, Heft 8, Stuttgart 1968, p. 66). To evaluate these results as compared with other findings which point in the opposite direction would require a thorough methodological discussion.
11. In Norway, in 1968, 2,055 persons were given unsuspended prison sentences for felonies, of these only 157 sentences were for more than one year, and only 8 for more than three years. Of more than 3,000 prison sentences for misdemeanors the great bulk were for less than three months. This sparing use of long prison sentences must, of course, be seen in relation to the peaceful social conditions of the country, with very little violent or professional crime. As an outside observer of the English scene, I have the impression that English courts go a long way to avoid sending people to prison, but that prison sentences often are much longer than we are used to in the Scandinavian countries.
12. Morton, The Function of Criminal Law (1962).
13. Garfinkel, *Conditions of Successful Degradation Ceremonies,* in: 41 American Journal of Sociology 420 (1956).
14. Barbara Wootton, crime and the criminal law (1963). Since Lady Wootton accepts the necessity of taking general deterrence into consideration (see op. cit. p. 40 and pp. 97–102) she can hardly be counted among those reformers who will substitute a pure system of individualized treatment for punishment, but the difference is not great, since she *normally* will give priority to the likely effect of the decision on the offender himself (p. 101).
15. Or, as I prefer to say, in accordance with Continental terminology, *general prevention.* This concept includes

not only the direct deterrent, but also the moral and habit-forming influence of criminal law. See chapter 2, p. 35, and *Appendix 1*.

16. In: SCANDINAVIAN STUDIES IN CRIMINOLOGY, Vol. 3, 9–21 (1971).

APPENDIX 1

General Prevention and General Deterrence: A Terminological Note

In continental legal literature the term "general prevention" is used as a technical term to signify the motivating
effect of the threat of punishment, whereas "special prevention" (or "individual prevention") is used to signify the
effects of actual punishment on the offender. General-
preventive effects include not only the motivating effects of
fear of punishment, but also the moral (or educative) and
habituative effects of criminal law.

   When I first published "General Prevention—Illusion
or Reality?" in 1952, I was not aware that the term general
prevention was virtually unknown in the English-speaking
world. Modern British and American authors instead
speak of general deterrence. When deterrence is taken in
its ordinary sense it excludes the moral and habituative
effect of criminal law. Sometimes deterrence is defined so
as also to include these effects of the penal system. In later
papers which were prepared for American journals and in
the title of this collection I have substituted this term.

   The terminological question is, of course, not a very
important one as long as the necessary distinctions are kept
in mind. In fact, neither general prevention nor general
deterrence are quite satisfactory. Prevention of crime is a

very broad concept, comprising measures such as better education, psychiatric counselling, safety devices to make crime more difficult, and so on. From a linguistic point of view, therefore, general prevention is a broad and loose term. In continental discussions, however, this does not seem to have created difficulties. The vagueness disappears when general prevention is used as a kind of shorthand expression for "the general-preventive effects of criminal law."

The objections to using general deterrence in the same sense are first, that it seems somewhat inconsistent with common usage to let deterrence comprise also moral and habituative effects, and second, that this terminology leaves us without a convenient expression for the purely deterrent effects as something different from the moral and habituative effects.

For the sake of convenience one often speaks about the general-preventive (or general deterrent) effects of *punishment*. It is more exact to speak about the effects of the *threat of punishment* or of *criminal law*. The threat is pronounced in the penal provisions, but the words of the law cannot be seen isolated from the machinery of justice. The threat of the law is demonstrated and made real by the activities of police, prosecution, courts, and prisons. Normally the threat of the law is directed towards all members of society. But some penal provisions are directed towards certain limited groups, for example civil servants, judges, doctors, military personnel, food-dealers, and so on. In these cases also we speak of general prevention (deterrence).

On the relationship of general and special deterrence I refer to *Appendix 2*.

APPENDIX 2

GENERAL AND SPECIAL DETERRENCE

Once a person has been actually punished he is still under the threat of the law but his motivation is more complex than before. He now knows what it is like to be prosecuted and punished, and this may influence him in various ways. The threat of the law alone was not sufficient to make him conform previously. If he is now deterred by the actual experience of punishment we speak of *special deterrence*.

In the case of serious crimes such as murder, rape, or armed robbery the number of convicted and punished offenders is very small in comparison with the total population. The experience of special deterrence will be an experience for the few. In the case of minor offenses, for example, traffic offenses, this is not so. Traffic law violations have been characterized as "a folk crime." [1] "Few drivers (and increasingly this means few adults) have never in their lives received a traffic summons, and even fewer can claim that they have never violated the law."

The effects of actual punishment are usually discussed in terms of *reform* and *rehabilitation*. For the moment I shall concentrate upon the *deterrent aspect*. How does the experience of actual punishment influence the deterrent effect of the threat—a deterrent effect which has proved, in this case, insufficient to prevent the offense?

Prima facie, it seems natural to expect that the experience of punishment would tend to strengthen fear. The abstract threat of the law has come to life, and the offender visualizes the consequences more clearly than he did before. In her book on department store shoplifting, Mary Owen Cameron vividly describes this mechanism in the arrested amateur shoplifter ("the snitch").[2] The investigation procedure of the store makes it increasingly clear to the pilferer that he is considered a thief and is in imminent danger of being hauled into court and publicly exhibited as such. This realization is often accompanied by a dramatic change in attitudes and by severe emotional disturbance. "This is a nightmare," said one woman pilferer who had been formally charged with stealing an expensive handbag. "It can't be happening to me. Why, oh, why can't I wake up and find that it isn't so," she cried later as she waited at a store exit, accompanied by a city and a store policeman, for the city police van to arrive. The professional shoplifter who has been arrested behaves quite differently. "He does, of course, make every effort possible to talk his way out of the situation. But once he finds that this is impossible, he accepts jail and its inconveniences as a normal hazard of the trade."

This description highlights several important points. It shows how the actual experience is much stronger than the theoretical knowledge. It further shows not only how fear might influence the future behavior of the shoplifter but also that he now realizes more clearly than before that he has committed a criminal and shameful act. The experience acts as a "moral eye-opener." Before arrest most shoplifters do not think of themselves as thieves, but this is brought home to them through arrest and investigation. Further, the description illustrates what a serious shock detection and arrest can be even if no prosecution, conviction, and sentence follow. "Among pilferers who are apprehended and interrogated by the store police but set free without formal charge there is *very little or no recidivism.*" [3] Whereas the threat of the law has not had a sufficient deterrent or moral effect, the actual experience of being caught has. The special-preventive effects are, in this situation, not due to legal punishment. But the institution of legal punishment looms in the background, giving the apprehension and investigation its dramatic impact and defining the risk connected with repetition of the crime.

The experience of being caught may also lead the offender to perceive the *risk* of detection and apprehension as greater than he did previously. In a study of drunken driving in Sweden, Klette asked a sample of automobile owners about their estimate of the risk for a drunken driver to be arrested under various circumstances.[4] The result was that drivers who had themselves been arrested for drunken driving had an estimate of risk many times higher than other drivers. This may be due to the common tendency to generalize from personal experience, and would thus hold true for other kinds of offenses.

We cannot, however, take for granted that the experience of punishment always tends to strengthen the offender's fear of the law. It may work the other way. It is conceivable that he has had exaggerated ideas of the consequences of being caught and now draws the conclusion that it was not as bad as he had imagined. More important, probably, is the fact that if a person has been convicted of a somewhat more serious crime, and especially if he was sentenced to imprisonment, he will have less to fear from a new conviction, since his reputation is already tarnished. In penological literature it is often asserted that the offender's fear of imprisonment is much reduced once he has become acquainted with it, but there does not seem to be any systematic research which could prove or disprove such assertions.

To complete the picture, it is necessary to mention the effect which, in psychological terminology, is called "reinforcement." When a person commits a crime his perception of the threat of punishment will change whether he is detected or prosecuted or not. If the criminal act leads to the envisaged goal and is not followed by unpleasant consequences this will normally reinforce his tendency to repeat the act. The psychological barrier which the fear of punishment represented will be weakened. If the act is repeated with the same result, further reinforcement will take place, and a criminal habit can be formed. The teller who has started to embezzle or the warehouseman who has started to steal from the stock, will tend to continue his activity until he is detected. This mechanism of reinforcement is probably especially strong if the crimes are committed in company with others who share the experience and give each other mutual support.

There is every reason to believe that detection and punishment have a deterrent effect in the majority of cases as compared with the alternative no detection and no punishment. And common sense would indicate that the deterrent effect increases in strength with the severity of punishment.

But, of course, to deal with the effects of actual punishment under the aspect of deterrence alone, is a too narrow perspective. Punishment may change the offender for better or worse quite apart from its deterrent or non-deterrent effects. The situation is very different for various penalties. A fine will not produce much effect other than a more or less pronounced deterrence. Much the same is the case with the short prison sentence. A radical personality change cannot be expected to take place through this kind of punishment. Whatever positive effect it may have, apart from the moral eye-opener effect described in the shoplifting example, is primarily as a deterrent.

The case is different and more complex with long-term imprisonment. The prison staff tries to train and reform the offender in order to release him from the prison as a better man than he was on his arrival. Both the day to day experience of the prison staff and sociological prison research in recent years show that the influence of fellow inmates often works in the opposite direction. The prisoner may leave prison as a worse man than when he entered, more deeply entrenched in a criminal culture, more hostile to society and its values, and less fit to meet the problems of a life in free society. Which of these opposite forces is, on the whole, the stronger? Although it has for generations been dogma in penology that short prison sentences represent a bad solution since they do not give real opportunities for rehabilitative work, there is little evidence that longer prison sentences give better results than short ones. Since a long sentence ought to have a stronger *deterrent* value than a short one, this seems to indicate that the negative influences during a prolonged stay in prison outweigh or at least neutralize the rehabilitative efforts of the staff. If this is correct, whatever positive effect prison may have on the prisoner's future conduct would also in these cases, be primarily the result of deterrence.

The situation is further complicated by the effect which conviction and sentence may have on the social status of the offender. The stigma attached to conviction and sentence may reduce his chances of getting work or being accepted in his previous social circle. The stigmatization which serves a useful social function in the process of general prevention is harmful as far as special prevention is concerned.

In practice it will be difficult or impossible to isolate the deterrent effects of the prison experience from other effects. Research into attitudes and motivation may give some clues, but it does not permit any statistical evaluation of the relative importance of various influences. If the prisoner does not relapse into crime we will not be able to tell whether this is due to a deterrent or a reformative effect of the prison, or if it might not have happened if no prison sentence had been imposed. What we can measure is how offenders perform after punishment, expressed in figures of recidivism. And here three main features stand out clearly.

1. If we look merely at recidivism rates after various kinds of treatment, the dominant pattern is: the more lenient the treatment the better the results. Fines or probation give better results than prison sentences, and short sentences give better results than long ones. But then the composition of these groups is different in regard to personal characteristics and criminality. The less severe cases receive the most lenient sentences, which is a different way of saying that the group with lenient sentences represents the better risks.

2. If we correct for these differences and use modern prediction techniques to compare groups which can be considered equally good or bad risks, the dominant feature of the results is that the overall differences between the various methods of treatment are small or nonexistent. It seems as if the personality of the offender and the social environment to which he is returning are of much greater significance for his future conduct than the differential effects of our various kinds of treatment. It is not easy to change people, at least when treatment is carried out against their will. From the point of view of the prison administrator this may seem a pessimistic and depressing fact. In a broader, political perspective, it is a fact which also has its positive aspects.

3. First offenders, that is offenders who have only one conviction and sentence, have a rather low rate of recidivism irrespective of sentence, but the recidivism rate increases sharply with the number of previous convictions. It thus seems as if the majority of offenders react positively to punishment but that there remains a hard core of offenders who are neither reformed nor deterred. In these

cases punishment fails. So, on the whole, do other methods of treatment.

Notes

1. Ross, *Traffic Law Violation: A Folk Crime,* 8 : 3 SOCIAL PROBLEMS 231 (1960–61).
2. CAMERON, THE BOOSTER AND THE SNITCH 161–67 (1964).
3. *Ibid.* 151.
4. Klette, *On the Functioning of the Swedish Legislation Concerning Drunken Driving* (mimeo.) 7.

APPENDIX 3

The Relevance of Psychological Research for Deterrence Theory

It is commonplace that general insights into man's emotional life provided by the progress of psychology as well as the insight into the processes of social interaction are indispensable to a realistic understanding of the possibilities of criminal law as a means of influencing attitudes and behavior. These insights exclude any simplistic and generalized conception of the subject. It seems, however, to be difficult to find research of direct relevance to the question of the general-preventive effects of a threat of legal punishment. The interest of psychologists has, for natural reasons, been more concerned with the effects of actual punishment than with the effects of threats of punishment. And the legal threat of punishment has special features which sets it apart from most other life situations:

1. The threat is *abstract* and *impersonal*. A man tempted to break the law is normally in a very different position than a man facing the command of another person. For this reason the highly interesting experiments in obedience by Milgram are of limited relevance to the problem of general-preventive effects of criminal law.[1]

2. The threat of punishment is normally directed against *forbidden activity*. It tries to motivate the individ-

ual to refrain from action. To put it in psychological terms, it is an "approach–avoidance" conflict. The psychological situation for a person who by threat of punishment is forced to do something is different than it is for a person who has to refrain from a certain activity. With respect to children the difference is described by Kurt Lewin.[2] Sometimes an omission is threatened with legal punishment, but provisions of this kind do not play an important role in criminal law.

3. The *character of legal penalties* differs vastly from the negative sanctions which are applied in psychological punishment experiments or commonly used in education or child upbringing. Legal penalties are not a succession of short and minor shocks or stimuli. In the case of a serious crime, it is a complex, painful, and long-lasting experience to be exposed to criminal justice. This is so even if the outcome is only a suspended sentence or probation, while a severe sentence for a serious crime can ruin a life. The other extreme is represented by the traffic ticket, which is much more like the kind of punishments ordinarily used in laboratory experiments or for educational purposes. The drastic character of the criminal process and the criminal sanction changes both the empirical and the ethical problems involved.

4. The threat of punishment is only *one factor* in a complicated motivational process in which personality factors, life situation, and nonlegal pressures combine in a highly varied way.

Criminologists who have been eager to apply the findings of psychological research to the problems of criminal law have sometimes overlooked these characteristics of the penal law. In recent years, papers have appeared in criminological journals which try to elucidate the problems of deterrence by reference to laboratory animal research. Thus one researcher finds that experimental evidence supports the classical school of criminology in its statement that it is the certainty of punishment—not the severity—that deters people from criminal acts; moreover, that a consequence must be applied immediately if it is to be effective.[3] The authors of another paper conclude that punishment is essentially an ineffective way of controlling or eliminating the behavior of the punished organism since the effects are usually transient and depend on continuous and repeated applications.[4]

These statements about the effects of punishment may or may not be correct in themselves. But certainly they cannot be deduced from the animal experiments upon which they are based. In the first place, these deductions overlook the basic distinction between the *threat of punishment* and *actual punishment*. Psychological animal research has been concerned with the effects of actual punishment. The general-preventive effects of criminal law, on the other hand, are achieved through the threat of punishment. The motivational situation is a very complex one; without a certain ability to think in symbols and adjust to future events the threat cannot work. The situation of a person facing the threat of punishment which criminal law attaches to a contemplated mode of action has nothing in common with the effect of electric shocks or other punishments administered to rats or pigeons following a certain behavior, for example, a pull on a lever or a peck on a disc. I think it can be confidently stated that animal research cannot make any significant contribution to the problems of the general-preventive effects of criminal law.

The situation is not very different with regard to the effects of actual punishment. The application of legal punishment is the result of the violation of a *general norm* which prescribes punishment and which the offender normally will know in advance. The whole experience derives its meaning from this relation between the general norm and the application of punishment in the individual case. The situation is very different from the situation of the confused rat or pigeon which is desperately trying to adapt its behavior to the incomprehensible manipulations of the psychologist. The experimenting psychologist describes as punishment any aversive stimulus such as electric shock or noise, which is explicitly arranged to follow a response.[5] It is doubtful whether there is any similarity at all, apart from the word punishment, to the situation of a human being undergoing punishment because he has committed an offense.

Moore and Callahan, in their well known study, *Law and Learning Theory,* take issue with the presupposition, supposedly held by jurists, "that the effect of a rule of law or of its administration is so different from the effect of all other devices affecting behavior that it is to be accounted for by a particular theory, applicable to law alone, and that the effect of law cannot be accounted for by a general theory of behavior which accounts for the effect of devices other than law." Their study, which was concerned with the effect of parking regulations and traffic signals under varying circumstances, tried to show that their findings were consistent with a general theory of learning, based on the four concepts "drive," "cue," "response," and "reward." It would be hard to disagree with the authors about the proposition that reactions to law and punishment constitute human behavior and therefore can be expressed in terms of a general theory of behavior. Moreover, the adherents of such a theory of behavior may find an intellectual satisfaction, a feeling of explanation, in being able to trace specific effects back to the general principles of the theory. But it follows from the very generality of the theory that it is not of much help in predicting the effects of a particular change in legislation, in law enforcement, or in sentencing. Since each situation is so specific, we have to rely on research designated specifically for this purpose. The contribution that a general theory could possibly make would be to provide a conceptual framework which could assist in clarifying questions and making them accessible to research. In this regard, the attempt of Moore and Callahan does not seem very rewarding. Its major contribution seems to be to describe simple findings in a complicated scientific terminology. That this study stands as an isolated effort more than twenty-five years after its publication indicates that this is a blind alley.

The psychological concept which seems to come closest to the way the problem of general prevention presents itself in criminal law is that of "anticipated punishment." Dollard et al. in their classic work, *Frustration and Aggression*, make this a key concept and refer to empiric research where the concept has been applied. It appears from the context that anticipation of punishment is to be expected as a result of previous experience of punishment: "Those actions cease to occur which, in the past, have been followed by punishment." Punishment is here, of course, taken in a wide sense including all kinds of painful responses from the social environment. The authors do not deal with the pure threat without actual experience of punishment. This may or may not be essential. Dollard et al. state as a law of behavior that *"the strength of inhibition of any act of aggression varies positively with the amount of punishment anticipated to be a consequence of that act"* (italics in original). This fits nicely with classical theories of deterrence and with common sense notions about the importance of the severity of a threat. But neither the enunciated principle nor the research which is adduced to substantiate it seem to be of much help in the difficult task of assessing what deterrent effects can be expected as a result of a contemplated change of policy.

In educational research, interest has been concentrated on the problem of whether punishment or reward is more effective as an incentive to moral and intellectual learning. In some fields of life a similar choice will be open to the legislator. Economic activities may be more conveniently regulated by creating a system of incentives than by legal commands and prohibitions. But in the traditional spheres of criminal law it will be impossible to institute a system of rewards for lawful conduct as an alternative to punishment. The legislator can attach penalties to theft, tax evasion, or speeding, but he cannot promise rewards to people who do not steal, do not give false information to the tax authorities, and keep within the speed limits. The religious preacher may promise Heaven to the obedient and Hell to the disobedient. The justice department has only the last possibility at its disposal.

The conclusion of this raid into foreign territory seems to be the following: Psychological theory and experiments may give suggestions, concepts, and research methods of interest to the lawyer who tries to assess the effects of criminal law or of a change in criminal law policy. I have no doubt that it would yield important results if psychologists devoted their interest to the effects of criminal law. But the questions are so specific that they ask for specific research. Analogies from experimental research may lead one astray if they are drawn without a clear conception of the differences between the life situation and the experimental setting.

Notes

1. Milgram, *Behavioral Study of Obedience,* 67 J. AB. Soc. Psych. 371–78 (1963); *Some Conditions of Obedience and Disobedience to Authority,* 18 Human Rel. 57–76 (1965).

2. Lewin, A Dynamic Theory of Personality (1935).

3. Jeffery, *Criminal Behavior and Learning Theory,* 56 J. Crim. L. C. & P. S. 295–300 (1965).

4. Appel & Peterson, *What's Wrong with Punishment?* 56 J. Crim. L. C. & P. S. 450–53 (1965).

5. Azrin, *Effects of Punishment Intensity during Variable-*

interval Reinforcement, 3 J. Ex. ANALYSIS OF BEHAVIOR 123–42 (1960).

6. Moore & Callahan, *Law and Learning Theory: A Study in Legal Control,* 53 YALE L. J. (1943).

7. DOLLARD ET AL., FRUSTRATION AND AGGRESSION (1939).

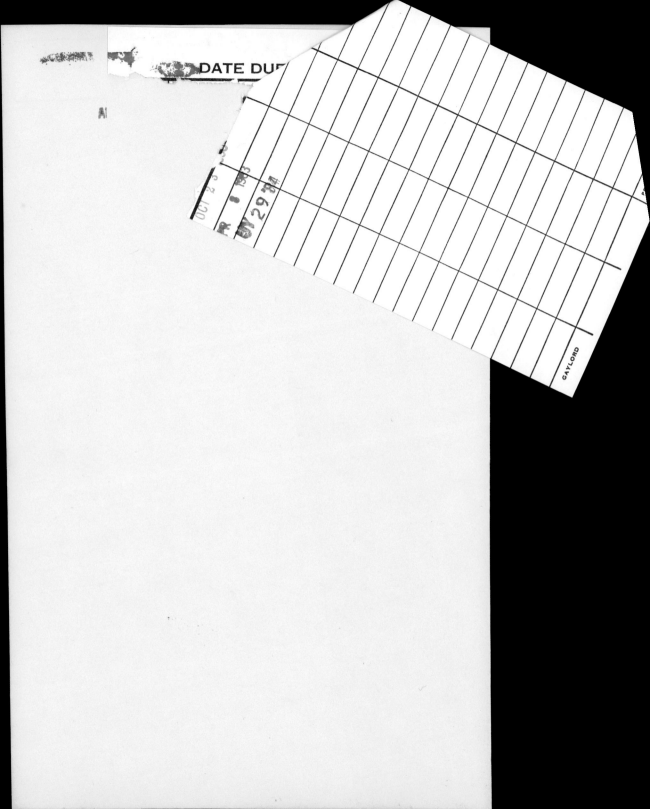